The Truth About Santa

The Truth About Santa

WORMHOLES, ROBOTS,
AND WHAT REALLY HAPPENS ON CHRISTMAS EVE

Gregory Mone

BLOOMSBURY
New York   Berlin   London

Published by Bloomsbury USA, New York

All papers used by Bloomsbury USA are natural, recyclable products made from wood grown in well-managed forests. The manufacturing processes conform to the environmental regulations of the country of origin.

LIBRARY OF CONGRESS CATALOGING-IN-PUBLICATION DATA
HAS BEEN APPLIED FOR.

ISBN-10 1-59691-618-4
ISBN-13 978-1-59691-618-0

First U.S. Edition 2009

3 5 7 9 10 8 6 4 2

Illustrations copyright © 2009 by Harry Campbell

Typeset by Westchester Book Group

To Nika

Contents

The Truth About Santa

Introduction

BELIEF IN SANTA CLAUS is fading. In some cities, children as young as sixteen are now rumored to be stomping home from school in the days leading up to Christmas and crying before their parents, "Why did you lie to me? Why did you tell me he was real?"

These confused young people shouldn't be blamed for their newfound doubts. On some level, Santa's annual rounds, and so many of the other details surrounding his operation, do seem impossible. Think about it. He knows if we've been bad or good. All of us. He also knows what we all want for Christmas, when we're sleeping, and when we're awake. To most people, that probably doesn't just sound implausible; it undoubtedly seems a little creepy, too.

The whole immortality issue usually spurs a few questions, too, especially since the legends suggest that Santa lives on a diet of milk and cookies. Normally, this sort of eating behavior leads to obesity, heart disease, and, in all likelihood, an early death. According to what we know about health and nutrition, Santa wouldn't make it to sixty, let alone six hundred.

Then there's his travel routine. Skeptics doubt that he's really able to traverse the entire globe in just a few hours via a reindeer-drawn sleigh. They scoff at the notion that reindeer can fly in the first place. They wonder how it is that Santa can slip down the slimmest chimneys despite his reportedly prodigious waistline. They laugh at the notion that he can do so while carrying a sack over his shoulder that somehow contains enough toys for most of the kids on the planet.

And how is it that he never makes mistakes? His sleigh never slips off one of those slanted, snow-covered rooftops and crushes some family's SUV in the driveway below. He never trips a security alarm or gets caught on video. You never see a camera-phone-captured clip of him on YouTube.

There are many arguments that attempt to refute the existence of Santa Claus. But they are all wrong. (Except for the reindeer one.) They are, in a word, uneducated. The problem with kids today, and the reason they are so quick to give up believing, is that they lack the basic knowledge of the universe required for a true understanding of Santa. As anyone with a decent grasp of physics, biology, and materials science understands, Santa's advertised abilities are perfectly plausible.

Yes, Santa is real, and this book will reveal, for the first time, how he completes his seemingly impossible annual mission. The simple answer? Technology. Santa has at his disposal some of the most advanced equipment, devices, materials, and means of transportation in this or any other universe.

The book will first address the origins of St. Nick and his operation, including Santa's true identity, whether or not he really completes all the deliveries himself, and why it wouldn't make sense for him to go the corporate route and outsource the whole business. Then we'll explore some questions about his health and explain how on-demand organ printers, intelligent robotic surgeons, and a hibernation-based antiaging program have helped him thrive despite his terrible diet.

We'll delve into Santa's ties to big business and the true nature of the North Pole, including its automated elf-cloning system and electricity-generating underwater turbines. The workshop has a massive server farm, too, which you'd have to expect given the amount of surveillance data Santa collects each year. He knows if you've been bad or good because he uses flying robotic spies.

And how does he move around the world so quickly? Think warp drive and wormholes. This book will detail the function of both, and also explain how Santa's suit doubles as an invisibility cloak and why all the gifts he deposits are either self-assembled under the tree or, in rare cases, teleported.

Of course, we'll also discuss some of the relevant psychological and sociological issues at the North Pole. For example, how the positively transcendent beauty of Mrs. Claus led Santa to reject the idea of cloning himself and why robots don't change diapers. If you're looking for the recipe for Mrs. Claus's eggnog, though, you will be disappointed. How she achieves such a perfect balance of cream, egg, and brandy we will never know.

PART I

Origins

Why Santa Can't Use FedEx

OUTSOURCING, CARBON-EMISSION-CANCELING SAPLINGS, AND OTHER COSTLY COMPLEXITIES OF DOING CHRISTMAS THE CORPORATE WAY

THE SCIENCE FICTION writer Arthur C. Clarke used to say that any sufficiently advanced technology is indistinguishable from magic. This is particularly relevant in the case of Santa Claus. For years people have attributed the successful completion of his annual rounds to magical tricks. Yet every one of Santa's amazing abilities comes from real technology. And he needs these fabulous gadgets, vehicles, and devices because it would be too hard for one man, or even millions of people, to accomplish his annual mission without them. It would be ridiculously expensive, too. How costly? A. T. Kearney consultant Mike Moriarty and his team recently looked at what it would take if Santa couldn't slow time or fly behind a set of reindeer but was instead powered by a bottomless bank account.

First, they decided that Santa would probably rely on the Internet. Using a mail room to collect wish lists, or even staffing a call center to speak with kids directly, would be too slow, costly, and complex. Moriarty suggested that instead of writing letters, kids would register for gifts on sites like Facebook, Club Penguin, or MySpace. There would be limitations, of course. Santa couldn't allow them to request a Ferrari or a window seat on the first space tourism plane. Parents and guardians would need to be involved. They would have to be able to check to make sure that little Robby wasn't asking for the Mature-rated game they already said he couldn't have. They could assist with the naughty-or-nice question, too, and help Santa determine whether a given child actually deserves a gift. Kids can't be trusted to assess their own behavior.

Moriarty concluded that Santa would probably want to steer a percentage of kids to virtual presents, such as gift cards, that could be fulfilled online. This way, he would have fewer presents to deliver and, as a result, lower costs and environmental impact.

What about those friendly little elves? Keeping them on the payroll all year wouldn't really make sense, from a business standpoint. No, Santa would outsource his toy manufacturing operations. This would save him serious money, but it would add another level of complexity. Santa has a reputation to uphold, a brand to manage, so he would have to ensure that all of these factories adhered to the best standards possible, in terms of working conditions, wages, quality of the goods. If you think Mattel looked bad after that lead paint was found in their toys, imagine what kind of public relations damage this would have done to Santa Claus. People would be cementing their chimneys shut.

The manufacturing facilities would have to be green. Given the risk that climate change poses to the North Pole—a topic to be discussed at length in chapter 13—Santa would want guarantees that every factory be as environmentally friendly as possible. He'd insist that they take advantage of recycled materials, reusable building materials, and alternative energy whenever possible.

Still, it's really the next step, moving all those toys from factories to homes, that would do the bulk of the damage to the atmosphere. Moriarty and his team concluded that Santa would have to avoid air freight whenever possible, though it's the fastest option, and move the goods via container ships, rail lines, and, eventually, old-fashioned delivery trucks. To offset all the fuel burned along the way, he suggested planting Christmas tree saplings along the tree line in Russia and Canada.

The budget for this entire endeavor would be absurd, especially if you add in delivery: not just getting these gifts to kids' doorsteps, but slipping them under the tree in the middle of the night. Completing this final step in the U.S. alone would call for millions of highly trained employees, probably former military operatives, breaking and entering repeatedly without being seen or heard. The domestic tally for an operation of this scale would cost in the range of $30 billion per year.

"There is good reason why Santa employs cost-free and happy elves in workshops that do not actually exist in physical reality and delivers gifts using relatively greenhouse-gas-neutral reindeer power," Moriarty concluded. "In addition to being nice, it saves Santa a bundle."

Where Santa Got All His Wonderful Tools

COSMIC STRINGS, WARPED SPACE-TIMES, ROTATING UNIVERSES, AND THE LIMITS OF TIME MACHINES

IN THE FOLLOWING pages, you're going to hear a lot about Santa's gadgets. How he uses miniature flying robots, advanced satellites, highly sensitive listening devices, and a warp-drive-powered sleigh that's capable of bending and twisting space-time to such an extent that it actually slips Santa and his reindeer out of the observable universe. But before we discuss how the jolly old elf uses these futuristic tools to deliver toys to every good girl and boy in the world in just a few hours, one glaring question needs to be addressed.

Where did he get all this stuff?

He could not have invented everything himself. If this were the case, he'd need to be both a ridiculously smart scientist and an unbelievably resourceful engineer. He would have had to devise $e=mc^2$ decades before Einstein. Then he would have had to sprint through the next century of advances in physics, biology, chemistry, and other fields, pushing his understanding of how the universe works, on a large and small scale, to the level of scientists working in, say, the twenty-third century.

And knowledge would just be the start. He would have had to apply all he knows to develop the actual tools. This is no small feat; rarely has our world seen this combination of thinker and tinkerer. Einstein's work with light quanta might have laid out the path to modern electronics, but he certainly didn't build any lasers or scanners himself. For Santa, it wouldn't have been enough to learn how wormholes, the theoretical shortcuts between one spot in the universe and another, might work. To use these wormholes to whisk himself from one living room to another in less than a second, Santa would have had to figure out how to generate, monitor, and maintain them, too.

All of which is completely implausible.

If Santa were really that smart, if he had really figured out relativity years before Einstein, there is no way he would have been able to resist publishing his results. Sure, he's saintly. But no real scientist can resist letting their contemporaries know when they've solved a cosmic conundrum. Isaac Newton kept the calculus to himself for a little while, but once Gottfried Leibniz started boasting about his development of that higher form of mathematics, Newton made a serious effort to ensure that the history books would credit him and not his German rival. If Santa had made all these discoveries, the approval-hungry scientist in him surely would have slipped his findings into a journal or two, to win the approval, if not the worship, of his peers.

It's clear, therefore, that someone, or something, provided Santa with the technology he needs. But who?

A visitor from the future would be a strong candidate, given that the tools Santa uses to complete his rounds have either been developed in recent years, should come to pass in the next few decades, or, in a few extreme cases, don't exactly have a due date but aren't prohibited by the laws of the universe as scientists understand them today. In other words, they're still in the pipeline. And yet here we are, with Santa cranking out and dropping off Christmas gifts at an apparently impossible clip.

This suggests the possibility that some twenty-third-century inventor living on Earth, or, if we burn out our current home, in an underground base on Mars, must have had, say, a warp-drive-related "Eureka!" moment while sitting in their bathtub. Given the likelihood of water scarcity in a future habitat of this sort, that bathtub might very well have been full of their own recycled, treated, and purified urine, but that presumably didn't bother them much, since it was probably fairly standard. And it certainly wouldn't have gotten in the way of their thinking.

Now, how would that urine-washed thinker's greatest work find its way back to the North Pole? Time travel? Maybe, but Santa couldn't

jump forward to the future on his own. This is a nice, clean idea—
"Hey, this whole reindeer-drawn-sleigh-through-the-snow, carving-my-
own-toys-by-hand thing isn't working, so I better visit the twenty-third
century to see if they've got anything better"—but it's just not tena-
ble. We know that Santa is not a science or engineering genius. Originally, he was a shipbuilder. (More on this in chapter 4.) He's good
with tools, but he doesn't have the brains to invent a time machine.

The other possibility is that a few people from the future hand-
delivered this goodie bag full of tech. To do so, they would have had
to time-travel; exactly how they'd do it is difficult to determine. Today
there's nothing like Doc Brown's flux-capacitor-enabled DeLorean in
Back to the Future, and no one is close to perfecting the centuries-
hopping phone booth blindly ridden into both the future and the past
by Bill S. Preston Esq. and the incomparable Theodore Logan. Modern time machines exist as equations; they are theoretical playthings
that physicists explore in the service of learning more about the theoretical underpinnings of the universe. By working to determine
whether or not the cosmos would allow a sufficiently advanced civilization to travel to the future or the past, these scientists learn more
about our world and the way it works.

The famous thinker Kurt Gödel, a colleague and friend of Einstein's when both were working at Princeton University, published
one of the first formal mathematical descriptions of time travel in
1949. In Gödel's version, the universe as described by Einstein's general theory of relativity could include paths called closed timelike
curves. Generally, these off-ramps would allow you to jump in a ship,
fly for a while, and end up right back where you started in space and
time. You wouldn't just go from Los Angeles, soar for a while, and
then land back in Los Angeles. You'd show up in L.A. at the same
time you left and seriously confuse airport security.

This isn't quite the brand of time travel we see in the movies, but
it could still be useful. Say you saunter into a meeting or class and find
that you're completely unprepared. If there were a closed timelike
curve nearby, you could bring your books, travel along it, study up en
route, and then get back to the same place and time fully prepared to
wow your colleagues or teacher. The hitch is that Gödel's model calls

for a cosmos that rotates, and astronomers have since discovered that the universe is actually expanding, not spinning. What an idiot.

For Santa's purposes, then, Gödel's version is out.

Still, there are other options. The physicist Frank J. Tipler has suggested that a massive, infinitely long, spinning cylinder could conceivably create these closed timelike curves. Princeton University's J. Richard Gott has described a setup involving a pair of cosmic strings—incredibly dense filaments left over from the formation of the universe.

Meanwhile, Amos Ori, a Technion University physicist, has been working on a more practical scheme. Most time-travel setups require exotic objects. Cosmic strings, special black holes, negative matter—the kind of stuff you can't really find at Home Depot. But Ori's version doesn't require any out-of-this-world ingredients. With his model, all you need to do is harness the power of gravity.

Granted, his time machine wouldn't be easy to build. Santa's friends from the future would need technology that manipulates gravity the way we mess around with light and magnetism. We have no trouble bending, focusing, and intensifying light using devices like lasers. That's easy. But unless you count video games such as Half-Life 2, which features a gravity gun that allows players to both attract and repel objects, we're not there yet with the force that brought the apple down on Newton's head. Gravity has proven to be a little trickier than light.

The big advantage of Ori's machine, from the getting-all-those-techie-toys-to-Santa perspective, is that it could allow travel to the distant past. With most time machines, that's not possible. They come with a very important caveat: You can't go back any further in time than the creation of the first machine.

Think of time travel like an airplane trip. You can't just build the departure runway. You need an arrival airport, too. You need somewhere to go, or else you'll just end up flying around for a while and then landing right back where you started.

What this means is that until someone on Earth figures out how to build a time machine, or how to bend and twist space-time enough to allow for one, we're probably not going to get any visits from citizens of the twenty-third century. We don't have anywhere for them to land.

Ori's design reveals a potential detour around this theoretical obstacle, but it's not exactly practical. He has said that if it's possible to warp space-time enough to create one of these time-traveling paths, then it's also conceivable that the universe has done this on its own. In other words, the cosmos may have already built a landing strip for us. If this were the case, then it would be possible to fly back to some distant time and place. Our twenty-third-century travelers could jump into their time-travel ship, fly through a warped region of space-time, and eventually pop out far in the past.

The trick, though, is that they wouldn't be able to control where and when they'd be going. Ori's scenario suggests that time travel to some era before the invention of the first time machine is possible, but there wouldn't be much flexibility. The idea that Santa's friends from the future would be able to even land on Earth, therefore, is seriously suspect.

All of which leads us to the only logical conclusion: Santa's technology is of alien origin.

3

The Aliens Who Love Christmas

THE SEARCH FOR EXTRATERRESTRIAL INTELLIGENCE, EXTRASOLAR PLANET HUNTING, AND A SUSPICIOUSLY SANTA-SHAPED GALACTIC CLOUD

THE GREAT THING about aliens is that we know almost nothing about them. We don't know if they have eyes and ears, whether they're bipeds, or if they have anything like ice cream, avocados, or even kielbasa where they live. Yet scientists are working hard to close this information gap.

The Search for Extraterrestrial Intelligence, or SETI, has been training radio telescopes on the heavens for years, listening for faint signals from distant worlds. Billionaire investor and Microsoft cofounder Paul Allen has made several major contributions to the group, including a reported $25 million gift supporting the design and construction of an advanced new telescope array that bears his name. (Given that his current investment firm, Vulcan, is named after an alien race, one could assume that his involvement isn't entirely selfless; he may be trying to find his home planet.) And scientists aren't just listening. They're actively looking, too. In the last decade, astronomers have begun identifying hundreds of planets located outside our solar system. In the coming years, using increasingly advanced and more sensitive observatories, they will be studying those distant worlds more closely, checking to see whether they have the characteristics necessary to support life, including water, a favorable atmosphere, sufficient protection from radiation, etc. Unfortunately it's not as simple as checking to see if anyone's waving back at us.

Scientists have not yet had contact with intelligent, Christmas-focused alien life, but there have been some encouraging signs. In 2007, astronomers using the European Space Agency's XMM-Newton observatory, a space-based telescope that picks up light in the X-ray frequency, identified a cloud of high-temperature gas in the Orion galaxy and pointed out that it vaguely resembled Santa Claus. Cynics might interpret this as an effort to attract media attention to their finding, which turned out to be less concerned with the peculiar shape of the gas cloud than its presence near an active star-formation region. But perhaps it really was a signal of some sort. A message from a benevolent, Christmas-loving species saying, "Hey, we're over here!"

Regardless of where they live or what they eat, we do know that the aliens who provided Santa with all of his technology are an incredibly advanced civilization. From an engineering standpoint they are far, far ahead of us.

But why did they get involved? What motivated them to single out a white-bearded, big-bellied man and outfit him with technology that granted him superhuman abilities? It may be that they are members of a supremely charitable society founded on the spirit of giving, and that they concluded, after discovering and observing our planet, that a person or figure whose sole purpose in life was to give to others, with no gain for himself, would have a significant effect on the way regular people lived. They may have reasoned that by giving someone the tools to deliver gifts across the world, they would accelerate the moral evolution of humanity. The spirit of Santa would spread, and mankind would become an enlightened species. Wars would end; tips would increase; drivers aiming for the same parking spot would stop and wave each other ahead, saying, "No, take it, it's yours."

Yet we also know that these aliens are highly intelligent, so this line of thinking can't be right. Sadly, the real answer is elusive. Scientists are only now learning about the big-picture characteristics of the planets these aliens may or may not inhabit. They certainly haven't begun delving into their psychological or cultural motivations for interfering with life on Earth.

Still, we do know something about the man these aliens chose, the man who would become Santa Claus. There is strong evidence that he was a shipbuilder named Jebediah Meserole, and that before moving to the North Pole, he lived in Greenpoint in Brooklyn, New York.

4

From Shipbuilder to Toy Maker

PERHAPS YOU'RE WONDERING how it is that Santa is from Brooklyn—specifically the neighborhood of Greenpoint. Indeed, this goes against the received wisdom. But that jumble of tales we know of as the Santa Claus story is heavily tainted with misinformation.

Until the mid-nineteenth century, Santa was a myth. A total fabrication. Sure, children had been receiving gifts all that time, but these items were actually provided by their parents. Santa was no more real than the tooth fairy or the Easter bunny. Of course, he was alive and well in stories and songs, paintings and pictures. He already had a detailed mythological history; he had appeared in various forms, in different cultures, for hundreds of years. Variations of him have turned up in Africa, Italy, Russia. Many people trace him back to Saint Nicholas, an immensely charitable man who lived in present-day Turkey in the third and forth centuries. He was a good friend to children, and earned the nickname Saint Nicholas the Wonderworker. His legend spread across the Western world, and, in fact, the name "Santa Claus" comes from the Dutch for St. Nicholas: Sinterklaas.

Eventually, the legend of Santa Claus became popular in America, too. Washington Irving wrote about Santa in his book *Knickerbocker's History of New York*, and Clement Clarke Moore crafted one of the more influential descriptions of Santa's routine in his seminal poem "A Visit from Saint Nicholas." By the early to mid-nineteenth century, all the stories, poems, and illustrations had begun to spawn imitators. Inspired by the legend, people across the world would try to carry out Santa's mission in their own towns, neighborhoods, and cities. Men would dress up in festive costumes, throw bags of presents over their shoulders, and break into their friends' and neighbors' homes to drop off toys. Granted, not all of them had charitable intentions. There were also a number of Santa-themed robberies at the time and a few isolated cases of adultery. (The famous lyric "I saw Mommy kissing Santa Claus" isn't actually about the big guy; the man that little kid saw was a neighbor disguised as Santa. Although she's aware of this misconception, Mrs. Claus still doesn't allow this song to be played at the North Pole.) Thankfully, though, these imposters and philanderers did not taint the growing legend, and there were far more warmhearted men at work than scurrilous ones.

Jebediah Meserole was one of these benevolent imitators. A resident of Greenpoint, Brooklyn, he worked by day as a shipbuilder. As a result, he had the woodworking skills required to craft nineteenth-century toys. He and his wife, who was so radiant that locals said she could make roses bloom just by looking at them, had no children of their own, but Meserole spent most of his nonworking hours building toys for local kids. And on Christmas Eve, staying true to the legend of St. Nick, he'd trudge through the snow from house to house, delivering these gifts. While this is all very interesting and warm and fuzzy, none of it constitutes hard evidence. In fact, the only serious proof that this man became the real Santa may have been destroyed.

In the mid-1970s, beneath a building on the corner of Nassau Avenue and Russell Street (the present-day location of Greenpoint's renowned Palace Café), a scientist from the Hercules chemical company found trace evidence of elements that had never before been seen on Earth. He concluded that the material had probably been deposited or discharged at some point in the mid-nineteenth century. Contemporary scientists were doubtful that this man had really discovered alien elements in Brooklyn, so they demanded evidence. The scientist was scheduled to bring samples to New York University, but the night before his appointment, a dozen pointy-eared, three-foot-tall men broke into his lab, stole all the material, and cleaned out the original site, too.

Needless to say, the report of that scientist was never published; his name remains a mystery, too. The key point here, though, is that the location of his dig was once the site of Jebediah Meserole's home.

Furthermore, based on his conclusions, those strange elements were deposited in that soil when Meserole lived there. More precise details have proven difficult to obtain, as Santa appears intent on keeping his original identity unclear, perhaps to prevent his descendants from asking for extra presents, but we can only assume that he dispatched those elves to erase the evidence.

Again, we don't know the aliens' real motivations, but it is perfectly logical to assume that once they arrived here on Earth, they studied the work of a few of the amateur Santas and chose one they deemed worthy of a much grander task. They must have picked Meserole, and informed him of their intention to give him the tools to spread Christmas cheer not just in his neighborhood, but across the world. Presumably, they told him that they could transform him into a real Santa Claus, a man with even more phenomenal capabilities than the figure of legend.

So, why was that evidence left behind? In all likelihood, Meserole asked for a demonstration of one or a few of these technological toys, and the aliens probably complied. Those trace elements discovered under Palace Café were probably exhaust from a warp drive.

This is all highly speculative, though, and for that I apologize. From here, however, the story is easy to piece together. After accepting the challenge, Meserole dropped his old name, moved to the North Pole with his wife, and became the real, the one and only, Santa Claus. With the help of those aliens, he transformed that centuries-old myth into reality.

And while Meserole was the Original Claus, or OC, it must not have been long before he realized that he would need help. Even with all his wonderful gadgets, Santa would never be able to drop off all the necessary presents himself.

5

Why Santa Needs Lieutenants

RELATIVITY, WORMHOLES, AND THE LOGISTICAL DRAWBACKS OF TIME TRAVEL

To GET A SENSE of the challenges posed by Santa's itinerary and, in turn, understand the absolutely inescapable need for assistants, let's look at the numbers. It's hard to estimate exactly how many presents Santa delivers on a given Christmas Eve, since the figure is constantly on the rise, but a conservative guess would be three hundred million. Many homes contain more than one gift-receiving child, which rounds the number of actual drop-ins down to two hundred million.

Now let's say that he gives himself thirty seconds inside each house. This means it would take him one hundred million minutes to deliver each and every gift. That works out to roughly 190 years with-out factoring in travel or the time it takes to get from one living room to the next. (In fact, he doesn't need to worry about this, since his op-eration relies on the theoretical shortcuts through space-time known as wormholes, which drastically reduce the house-to-house commute. A wormhole that's merely a few meters long can connect two points that are millions of miles away from each other.) Given these figures, and without counting transit time, Santa would need almost two cen-turies to finish a single night's worth of deliveries.

Granted, he could time-travel via methods discussed in chapter 20. The aliens did give him the requisite technology, and since he wouldn't be headed for the distant past, he wouldn't encounter the same obstacles as our hypothetical friends from the future. But this technique would only save him seconds and hours relative to all those sleeping boys and girls. Think of it this way: If he visits a house at midnight, spends his thirty seconds dropping off gifts, and then jumps into one of his time machines, goes back thirty seconds while moving from one spot to the next, and arrives at his destination at midnight again, he hasn't lost a millisecond. That is, the night hasn't advanced, and he's no closer to his four thirty A.M. deadline, at which point all of the toys in a given time zone must be in place.

Yet for Santa himself, the thirty seconds he spent in that first house are real. His body's clock has already advanced and can't be wound backward. Sure, time machines would allow him to deliver all those presents in the necessary nine hours. Technically he could even finish the job in a second's worth of our time, if he chose to. But he would never get back the half-minute spent in each home. Those in-tervals would still add up, and Santa would be about 190 years older after a single night of deliveries, even if only a second had passed on Earth. If Santa's system really did work this way, he'd be tens of thou-sands of years old today. And immensely bored, no doubt.

Ah, but what if he were to use the time machine each year to go back to a few minutes before he started, pop into the Pole, and tell his younger self, "Hey, don't worry about it, your deliveries are all done"? His younger self could then skip the night's work and wake up on

Christmas morning just a few hours older than when he went to sleep, instead of having 190 extra years tacked on to his chronometer.

Unfortunately, this wouldn't really work, either, for a number of reasons. The theoretical implications of this problem are addressed in chapter 21, but think of it this way: If his younger self were to go to sleep, he'd never deliver those presents or get in the time machine afterward to tell himself to take the night off. Besides creating a cosmic conundrum that might lead to the destruction of the universe, or at the very least the onset of a migraine for anyone who bothers thinking too much about this sort of thing, his actions would result in millions of kids hustling excitedly into their living rooms the next morning to find themselves a few presents short.

So. No matter how much technical trickery is applied, the notion of a single Santa Claus just doesn't compute. An operation of this scale needs employees, stand-ins, mindless wage slaves. And Santa has them. Between two and three hundred, in fact. The number varies, as these lieutenants only work on short-term contracts and occasionally become the unlucky victims of malfunctions in his wormhole-based time machines, which have a relatively rare but very unfortunate tendency to leave their pilots adrift in alternate universes. (In all likelihood, these are fatal accidents, but because it's impossible to extract information from alternate universes, Santa comforts himself, and his subordinates, by assuming that they've been adopted by a margarita-loving alien race that lives on a planet with a UV-blocking atmosphere that allows them to sunbathe all day without ever contracting skin cancer.)

Who are these men? Are they clones of Santa himself? That would make sense on some level. They would fit into his clothes and shoes, so he could loan them old or worn-out uniforms. And if he were to play cards with them, Santa would probably know their poker faces, since they'd also be his face. Santa even has the necessary cloning technology. Ultimately, though, Santa decided against creating knockoffs of himself because he didn't want one of his doubles romancing Mrs. Claus. If you saw her, you'd understand. She could melt a polar ice cap quicker than global warming. And their relationship has not always been so solid. Back in Brooklyn, the former Jebediah Meserole came home from the shipyard more than once to find a local farmer leaving his humble home with a relaxed smile on his face. Initially, he used the old "ho, ho, ho" refrain despondently; it was something he muttered sadly under his breath. Only later, after Meserole's transformation into Santa Claus strengthened their marriage, did it become a cheerful rallying cry.

So, instead of cloning himself and potentially endangering his marriage, Santa recruits normal folk to be his lieutenants. Each of these Santas, with the use of a wormhole-based time machine and numerous other alien technologies, spends approximately six months delivering presents every Christmas Eve. Again: That's six months in their time; for the rest of us, the time-machine-free citizens of the here and now, just a few hours elapse. Following those deliveries, they live a time-travel-free year at the Pole, with two ten-day vacations, one to Vegas for a critical, Christmas-related convention, and another, just prior to the big night, to the Four Seasons Hualalai, on the big island of Hawaii. The logical conclusion here would be that in a given year, they actually age eighteen months, but Santa's hibernation program—a sleep-pod-based system, reviewed in chapter 10, that halts aging in patients—actually cancels out a large portion of that time, from a getting-older perspective.

Of course it's all for a good cause, but you're no doubt wondering why anyone would want to take such a job. Even with that extended respite and the two luxurious annual vacations, working like a galley slave for six months takes its toll on the body and mind. But there are also plenty of benefits. If they don't get lost in an alternate universe, these men are likely to retire with a deliciously large sum of money in the bank. We'll detail the compensation structure in part 3, but there's another benefit that's equally alluring.

Santa offers a fantastic health plan.

PART II

Health

6

Santa's Shrinking Waistline

THE OBESITY EPIDEMIC, RNA INTERFERENCE,
AND THE MYTH OF THE FAT, JOLLY ELF

A MASSIVE WAISTLINE, a jiggling belly, and a fat, ruddy face have long been essentials of the Santa Claus aesthetic. These physical characteristics were part of the Santa myth long before Jebediah Meserole and his alien friends turned that legend into reality. Meserole himself tended toward the spherical, and when he abandoned his normal life and became the OC, he was intent on maintaining his girth. The people liked a fat Santa? He'd make sure they got one. He shifted to a diet consisting primarily of eggnog, whole milk, and chocolate-chip cookies. He wanted his lieutenants to be similarly large, so when he began recruiting, he only interviewed prospective employees with size-44-and-up waists.

There were technical drawbacks to this hiring strategy. For one, it capped the number of homes his lieutenants could visit via wormhole, for reasons detailed in chapter 20. But the real problem with Santa's insistence on prodigious waistlines had less to do with operational logistics than world health. In recent years, obesity has grown from a problem into an epidemic. Nearly one-third of American schoolchildren are overweight. Sixteen percent of kids between the ages of two and nineteen are obese. Back in the 1970s, only 5 percent of children in the same age bracket fell into that category.

This is bad, of course, because obesity increases the risk of diabetes, heart disease, and some types of cancer. It can also affect mental health. An analysis of grade-schoolers in Korea concluded that severely overweight children have lower self-esteem. Several studies have linked obesity to depression, and still others contend that it's linked to migraines and chronic headaches. A group of researchers at the University of Texas even attacked the old "fat and happy" idea directly. They found that for eight different indicators of mental health, including happiness, life satisfaction, and optimism, obesity either had no effect or made people worse off. The overweight, they concluded, are no more jolly than their wispy brethren.

Granted, we can't blame the rise in obesity entirely on Santa Claus and his support of large waistlines. Numerous factors, both genetic and environmental, have driven the trend. Children and adults have shifted to a more sedentary, TV-and-PC-focused lifestyle, and until recently, there was far too little focus on nutrition. But you can imagine that Santa didn't feel too great about himself or his position as a role model when he became aware of the obesity problem. So, in 2002, after numerous consultations with branding experts, policy makers, scientists, and, just because he thinks they're funny, semioticians, Santa decided to shrink his waistline.

For the average person, this sort of decision would be followed by a drastic change in lifestyle. But Santa and his lieutenants didn't need to change their diet, and the OC didn't have to order a few hundred elliptical machines for the North Pole, either. No, all they had to do was pop a few pills.

South of Santa's workshop, down here in the non-alien-technology-enhanced world, weight loss is hardly this simple, but recent research points toward groundbreaking new means of fighting fat. In 2005, Jonathan Graff of the University of Texas–Southwestern reported that a gene called adipose may serve as a master regulator of fat levels in our bodies. In one experiment, Graff found that increasing adipose activity in mice allowed them to gorge on food and still remain lean. A different set of mice with dialed-down adipose activity gained weight on a similar diet. Graff determined that the gene doesn't just act as a simple on/off switch, instructing the body to either burn or store fat. It's more of a volume dial. The more you crank it up, the more fat you convert into energy.

Other scientists have found that shutting down specific genes could have fat-fighting potential. In 2006, a group led by biologist Michael Czech at the University of Massachusetts reported that they'd used a technique called RNA interference to silence the gene RIP140. RNA interference interrupts a cell's signaling system; it stops proteins from doing the work determined by their corresponding genes. When Czech used it to switch off RIP140, a host of other genes involved in the cell's energy production process became far more active. In effect, knocking out the gene turned adipose cells into fat burners instead of fat accumulators. Czech showed that mice lacking RIP140 didn't gain weight even when fed a high-fat diet.

Santa's weight-loss program takes advantage of these and other forms of genetic trickery, keeping the OC and his lieutenants trim despite their shared penchant for dipping still-hot chocolate-chip cookies into chilled glasses of creamy eggnog. (The nog coats the freshly baked cookie, wrapping it in a blanket of fatty, alcohol-enhanced wonder . . . oh, if she would only reveal her recipe.) Now, if losing weight is so easy for Santa, the next question is why hasn't he just given this technology to the rest of the world? Obesity is an epidemic, and Santa has the means to help people lose weight. So why isn't he dropping his pills off on Christmas Eve instead of a bunch of toys and dolls?

Besides the risk of lawsuits, the widespread use of this technology, without an accompanying change in diet and lifestyle, could generate more problems than it would solve. Knowing they could burn fat on demand, people might switch to all-ice-cream diets and develop new and more complex ailments.

Which brings us to yet another question: How is it that Santa carried around all that weight for so long but remained vibrant and healthy enough to work like an industrial robot for one night a year? Forget that: How is it that the old guy is even alive?

7

How Santa Handles His Booze

LIFE EXTENSION AND DIETARY FLEXIBILITY
THROUGH ON-DEMAND ORGAN PRINTING

ALL THOSE YEARS of washing down mouthfuls of chocolate-chip cookies with cold glasses of creamy eggnog produced irreparable damage to Santa's organs. Particularly his heart. Think of the cholesterol, the fat, the sugar. The average circulatory system couldn't handle a habit like that for a decade, let alone a century.

The well-chronicled act of putting his finger aside his nose also indicates some heart-risky behavior. Was this really a way of whisking himself up the chimney? Or was it a sign that he'd just ingested a certain powder that kept him jolly and energetic through the night? We don't know. His lungs may have suffered, too. In early nineteenth-century depictions, before the famous illustrator Thomas Nast lifted his pencils to the task of sketching Santa, the old elf was never without his pipe. He appears to have smoked incessantly on his Christmas Eve rounds.

True, we know that these renditions aren't necessarily accurate. They're the product of legend, rumors, speculation, imagination. But they also stem in part from observations of the real Santa Claus, since the OC does allow select children to spot him on Christmas Eve. Furthermore, we know that there was a kind of feedback mechanism at play around this time: The legends influenced the OC, and his adoption of the characteristics he preferred, such as that hefty waistline, fed the pictures. If artists were drawing him with a pipe, then it's possible that the OC figured it would be okay for him to smoke on his rounds.

Despite these indulgences, Santa has managed to dodge lung cancer, emphysema, and numerous other diseases. This isn't because his organs are particularly special. The trick is that he gets to replace them. When Santa needs a new heart, he just has one printed.

His organ printer may actually be among the least fantastical of Santa's gadgets. Several scientists are trying to develop the technology today. Biophysicist Gabor Forgacs leads a team at the University of Missouri–Columbia that uses three-dimensional printers capable of making structures out of living cells. The group has already shown that its technique should be able to produce working sections of blood vessels. In the long run they hope to be able to print out the functional equivalent of bladders, hearts, livers, and more.

The printer works a little bit like a standard office ink-jet, with some key substitutions and modifications. In lieu of letterhead, the group lays down a gel-like material they call biopaper. And where the heads of your office printer spit out ink, Forgacs's machine dispenses tiny spheres packed with different cells. In some cases, the spheres harbor more than forty thousand individual cells. The concept is fairly simple. The machine prints a given structure from the bottom up, as if it's stacking blocks. To make a cylindrical blood vessel, for example, the group starts by printing the cell-filled spheres in a circular pattern on the first layer of the biopaper. Then they lay down another sheet and print out a second ring, right atop the first one. They continue the process, and the spheres eventually fuse, the vessel matures, and the cells actually start to organize themselves. This is nature's own little trick, and it saves Forgacs and his team quite a bit of trouble, since they don't have to figure out how to get the right cells to go to the right spots. The ones that belong in the outer wall migrate that way, and the cells that should be on the inside find their own way as well.

How long it will take these scientists to perfect their technology and extend its capabilities from blood vessels to functional substitutes for hearts and livers is an open question, but the fact that Santa has a versatile organ printer of his own should, at minimum, be encouraging to the rest of us.

Still, a printer is only one piece of machinery. It can't tell Santa when his heart is failing or when a lieutenant's liver is starting to shut down from too much brandy-and-rum-infused nog. Furthermore, how would he switch that ailing liver for a new one? A good question. But the answer should be fairly obvious.

Robots.

8

Robotic Surgeons in Silly Outfits

TELEOPERATION, ARTIFICIAL INTELLIGENCE, AND AUTONOMOUS MOBILE MANIPULATION

ROBOTS HAVE ALREADY become valuable members of operating rooms across the world. By early 2008, the da Vinci system, a surgical robot that's controlled by a live doctor standing nearby, had been installed in more than eight hundred hospitals in the U.S. The NeuroArm, a more recent development, will enable surgeons to carry out procedures in delicate areas such as the brain. Each of these machines takes advantage of something called teleoperation.

What this means is that a human actually runs the robot and makes all the key decisions. The doctor operates a pair of controllers while looking through a stereo viewer. When they move the controllers, a computer processes this action and instructs the robot's manipulators to move in exactly the same way. The surgeon becomes a puppeteer.

However, a setup like the da Vinci system doesn't lack intelligence. If the surgeon's hands shake a bit, the system will eliminate that flaw and hold its own instruments steady. Yet the bulk of the procedure is still being carried out by a person. And every time that person moves the controllers, a certain amount of information has to travel from the teleoperation apparatus to the robot that's actually poking around inside the patient.

This works perfectly well in an operating room when the surgeon is right next door and the information doesn't have to travel very far. It would even work fine over larger distances. The Pentagon, for example, is exploring a da Vinci upgrade that would allow doctors to operate on patients on the battlefield from a hundred miles away. Injured soldiers would be carried into a mobile, enclosed, robotic operating room, and the doctors, working in a safe zone far away, would use a future version of da Vinci to examine and possibly patch up their wounds.

Given that Santa and his lieutenants don't require new organs all that often—two procedures a year, at most—teleoperation would seem like a perfectly reasonable option. When necessary, you'd think that Santa's alien friends could perform the surgery, implanting a new liver or kidney remotely.

Unfortunately it's not that simple. We don't know exactly where these aliens live, but it's certainly not in our solar system. Teleoperation wouldn't work, therefore, because the commands would have too far to travel. Even performing the surgery from Mars would be out of the question, because it would take the necessary commands around ten minutes to get from the telemanipulator to the robot that's actually performing the surgery at the Pole.

Imagine Santa on the operating table, a robotic surgical system poised above him, Mrs. Claus and the elves sitting nervously in the other room. If something goes wrong during the surgery, news of that error, which travels at the speed of light, will take ten minutes to get back to the surgeon on Mars. And even if our alien operator knows how to correct it immediately, the first step in that fix won't happen for another ten minutes. In other words, a minimum of twenty minutes will pass before the problem occurs and the solution is set into play. That kind of lag wouldn't bode well for Santa.

Which is exactly why the aliens provided him with a group of autonomous, or independent, robotic surgeons. In the non-alien-assisted world, Duke University bioengineer Stephen Smith recently announced results suggesting that autonomous robotic surgery—operations without the doctor performing every move—isn't all that far-fetched. Using an advanced ultrasound imager that generates thirty pictures per second, creating detailed three-dimensional maps of interior structures, Smith showed that if given quality information and outfitted with artificial intelligence, robots should be able to complete simple surgeries without any help. The 3-D ultrasound map gives the robot a precise picture to work with, in the same way that laser scanners mounted on robotic cars give those vehicles' computers a map of the terrain they need to navigate. In one simulation, Smith and his colleagues showed that their robot and its ultrasound eyes had the skills to carry out a tumor biopsy.

Since Santa's robots are entrusted with far more complex tasks, including removing and inserting organs, valves, arteries, and more, they are outfitted with far more advanced artificial intelligence, computing power, and sensors. They don't simply activate a surgery program and follow a series of steps. Using ultrasound, stereo cameras, and more, they constantly monitor the environment—Santa's innards—assess whether any important changes have occurred, such as a blood vessel popping, and then decide how to respond to those changes, if necessary.

They are extremely intelligent machines, given these capabilities, yet they are not conscious. If they were, they would probably refuse to wear the candy-striper uniforms that Mrs. Claus made for them. You know, just to keep up the spirit. Call her strange, but let's be honest here: If you had a highly intelligent robot in your home, wouldn't you dress it up in silly clothes? Yes, you would. And besides, the elves—the ones who seem so perfectly suited for funny little costumes—absolutely refuse to wear even remotely demeaning or festive garments.

9

The Immortality Paradox

THE NEW SCIENCE OF AGING AND THE QUEST
FOR THE TWO-HUNDRED-YEAR LIFE SPAN

THE AVAILABILITY OF robust, replaceable organs, and robotic surgeons with the skills to switch them in and out, has certainly prolonged Santa's life. Still, we don't know if he's actually immortal. You could argue that angle, given that he is still alive. As my pleasantly wise great-aunt used to say, "The only way to prove someone's mortal is to kill 'em." But Santa has already lived for a phenomenally long time, which suggests that he must have other medical tricks. New organs alone couldn't account for his tremendous success in combating the effects of aging.

Today, scientists are working to extend the life spans of laboratory worms and mice, with an eye toward applying the tricks to humans, and possibly giving the rest of us a few extra years on Earth. Most researchers don't seem to think that anything approaching immortality, or a two-hundred-year life span, is within the grasp of modern science. The English biogerontologist Aubrey de Grey disagrees, but he's not like most researchers. He entered this particular field through an unusual door, earning his Ph.D. after proposing a slew of strange, wildly optimistic ideas about how to end aging. He also sports a frightening beard and looks like he'd be more comfortable ending lives, not extending them.

De Grey is developing a seven-step plan for ending aging that he calls Strategies for Ending Negligible Senescence, or SENS. It has been derided by some scientists and hesitatingly supported by others. The seven-step-ness of de Grey's approach immediately shouts self-help claptrap, but, unlike standard self-help books, his SENS plan does not lack detail. For example, one of the steps in his plan involves cleaning out the machinery in our cells known as lysosomes. These effectively act as waste recyclers: They pull in the cell's garbage, break it down, and spit it back out again in more useful form. Over time, though, de Grey says that these lysosomes become less efficient. They start accumulating mangled and unfamiliar forms of cellular waste that they can't operate on. The effect is a bit like bringing a bunch of newfangled soda bottles to the supermarket recycling machine, only to find that they don't fit. The machine doesn't take them, so they can't be recycled, and you've got to hold on to them and use them to construct a pyramid to impress your friends.

But we're getting off topic. The point here is that de Grey thinks the buildup of this cellular junk over time is one of the factors that contributes to the aging process in our bodies. As a result, he has essentially been trying to devise a way to dispose of the bottles that our cellular recycling machine can't deal with. He thinks that if you could clean out the lysosomes and crank up the efficiency of the recycling system, you might help stop the body from growing old.

If Santa were to use a SENS-like program, then the lysosome-cleaning process would likely involve periodic injections. Each shot would deliver a selection of enzymes capable of safely finding their way into Santa's cells and then into the specific machinery. Once inside, they would break down the trash that his own cells couldn't handle and help keep him fit as a forty-year-old. But that's a big if. The reality is that we don't know whether Santa or his lieutenants actually uses a SENS-like program, though the variety and quantity of pills they take and injections they receive hardly rules out the possibility.

In fact, it may be that another one of his programs has a greater impact in terms of extending his life span. Santa's hibernation system may be an even more powerful weapon in his battle with aging.

10

Why Santa Hibernates

HIBERNATION IS ONE of nature's strangest phenomena. Various mammals enter into prolonged, comalike states to last through the winter. This helps them deal with cold temperatures and limited resources; typically there just isn't enough food around in those months to support their normally active lifestyles. Hibernating mammals can drop their body temperatures to just above freezing, reduce oxygen consumption to anywhere from one-thirtieth to one-fiftieth of what they typically require, even slow their heartbeats down from hundreds to just three to ten ticks per minute. The core temperature of the Arctic ground squirrel actually drops below freezing.

When the cold months pass, these animals just jump right back up again without missing a step. All their nerves and neurons fire as they did before. Their organs resume their normal duties. Their muscles return to work despite months of torpor. They wake up as if from a long nap.

The idea of human hibernation has always fascinated science fiction writers and personal-injury lawyers. The latter fantasize about clients who incur injuries in automobile accidents, then agree to hibernate afterward, in order to exaggerate the apparent severity of those injuries and appear as if they've entered into a coma, which, in turn, would allow the attorneys to collect larger settlements.

But it's not just lawyers and writers who are drawn to the idea. Real-world researchers have explored the science of hibernation for at least a century. In the 1980s, NASA looked into human hibernation as a means of avoiding some of the problems that would be associated with long-term spaceflight. If you were to put astronauts to sleep during the eighteen-month trip to Mars, for example, they would require less food and water, and they wouldn't argue, fight, or have sex with one another. The motivation here mirrors Santa's rationale for putting his lieutenants to sleep. The aliens presented the hibernation program as an option, and Santa chose to put it in play for some very simple reasons.

The lieutenants spend most of the year with Santa and Mrs. Claus up at the North Pole. Keeping more than two hundred men in a confined space, with no access to the outside world and no contact with women, for ten months, would be absolutely foolish. Remember, Santa opted against cloning himself because he feared that one of his genetic twins would pop in Bing Crosby's "White Christmas" and swing Mrs. Claus right into his heart.

Naturally, then, the OC would also worry about the possibility that one of his lieutenants would do the same. Sure, he has come to trust his wife since they left Brooklyn, and he could ask his men to take a vow, sign a contract, etc. But after ten months underground, a few of them would undoubtedly neglect the agreement. Call him paranoid, but Mrs. Claus is a special lady. She's kind of hot, actually.

At the same time, Santa's hibernation program may not just be about keeping his jolly lieutenants from sneaking into his candy-cane-and-tinsel-adorned bed. He hibernates too, and his motivation may stem from the apparent antiaging effect.

In 1981, Harvard biologist Charles Lyman published a study that tested this idea on 288 Turkish hamsters. Each hamster was placed in its own cage, provided with food and water, and exposed to ambient light and natural day/night cycles. Half the animals were kept at a constant, warm temperature throughout the experiment, but the others were exposed to much colder air, starting in November and lasting through the winter. Lyman's idea was to simulate the onset of winter, which triggers hibernation in most mammals. It worked, and in the end, the hamsters that hibernated effectively lived longer than their counterparts, and nearly by the amount of time that they stayed under. In other words, the work hinted that these deep sleeps might delay the aging process.

Hibernation research didn't exactly stop with Lyman's paper, but it has gone through varying periods of interest and neglect.

NASA's need to figure out human hibernation was not so pressing, given that the agency isn't sending any crews to Mars in the near future, so the program was dropped. But now it's becoming an increasingly active area of research again. Matt Andrews, a biologist at the University of Minnesota, says this stems in part from the fact that scientists are no longer just observing mammals in this state or studying the external cues that initiate and halt the process. Now they're starting to explore hibernation at the molecular level. They're beginning to figure out what's happening on the cellular scale that enables animals to hibernate in the first place.

One of the most exciting findings: The creatures that do hibernate through the winter might not be specially equipped, in a genetic sense. Instead, hibernation-related genes might be common to all mammalian species. It's possible that bears, squirrels, and the rest are just the only ones putting them to work. Even humans most likely have the genetic machinery. "The genetics hardware is there," according to Andrews, "but it's the regulation of these genes, the turning them on and off, that's so very different between us and the natural hibernators."

Andrews and other scientists hope that studying the biological mechanisms behind animal hibernation could help with human problems. For example, organ transplantation. Today, an organ that's removed from a donor has only a limited shelf life, in some cases as few as four or five hours. But if scientists could isolate the proteins and enzymes that work to keep hibernating mammals' organs in perfect shape during long periods of inactivity by burning fat, conserving glucose, and performing other molecular tricks, they might be able to apply these findings to human hearts and livers. They might be able to figure out a way to store these precious organs for much longer and increase the chances that the neediest patients receive them.

Interest in human hibernation has also intensified thanks to a number of strange, almost impossible-sounding medical cases. In 1995, German scientists reported that a four-year-old boy who had accidentally fallen through ice into a freezing lake was successfully brought back after his heart had not ticked for eighty-eight minutes. His core temperature had dropped down to 67.6 degrees Fahrenheit, and none of the standard resuscitation measures had any effect. A medical rescue team was on the scene relatively quickly and evacuated him by helicopter to a hospital. But his heart didn't even register a beat until he'd been there for a full twenty minutes. Eventually, though, the boy recovered completely.

Such cases are rare, but a new one of these miracle recoveries does seem to turn up in the journals every few years. A Japanese toddler bounced back after a similar icy plunge; his heart reportedly stopped beating for thirty minutes. Then there's the story of Mitsutaka Uchikoshi, the famous Bear Man of Japan. He was lost for twenty-four days on an icy mountain in 2006. When he was found, his organs seemed to have shut down. His body temperature had dropped to 71 degrees. His pulse was nearly undetectable. He appeared to be dead. He should have been dead. Yet he, too, survived.

While these extreme cases imply that hibernation might be able to put life on hold, they hardly suggest a recipe for an antiaging program. Even Santa's ever-so-dedicated lieutenants, who give up so much and work so hard to support the spirit of Christmas (and earn the bonus they're due at the end of each term, along with a fresh new organ or two), would probably revolt if Santa's robots threw them out in the snow so they could sleep through the winter.

No, the Pole's hibernation system is far more user-friendly. Santa and Mrs. Claus choose not to hibernate for the full eleven-month term that the lieutenants endure. They prefer to spend a few months at the Pole with just the elves and robots for company, then travel for a few more, mostly via cruise ship, before hibernating for sixteen to twenty weeks. But this has less to do with the hibernation process itself than their desire to spend more time together.

To start the process, the subject reclines in a kind of sleep pod. His core temperature is reduced, his pulse slowed, his metabolism decelerated, his brain activity wound down. An IV, administered by robotic surgeons, provides limited sustenance. His organs continue functioning, though they're not nearly as active, and, as a result, he wears diapers.

(The technology embedded in the diapers, including a water-attracting, or hydrophilic, nanomesh structure that sucks in and purifies urine, makes the latest Huggies models look like simple paper towels. One can only assume, given the level of complexity of the materials, that the aliens themselves wear diapers and that they do so long past child-hood.)

The robotic surgeons refuse to change the hibernating Santas; it's not clear why. But it can't have anything to do with pride, given that they have no qualms about wearing the silly outfits Mrs. Claus makes for them. The changing job, therefore, is left to our poor little pointy-eared friends, the elves. They don't particularly enjoy this task, and more than one elf has, as both a form of protest and as a means of seeking appreciation for the gruesomeness of the assignment, applied in the last few years to be the subject of an episode of Mike Rowe's *Dirty Jobs*. As of 2008, however, the producers of that Discovery Channel show had failed to respond to their queries.

PART III

Santa Inc.

11

The Strategic Elvis Convention

HOW SANTA GENERATES REVENUE

THOUGH THE ALIENS provided Santa with plenty of technology, they did not equip him with much cash. This wasn't important at first, because Santa started small. Initially he limited his rounds to several hundred homes and completed all the deliveries himself. He didn't have any employees besides the elves, who essentially work for free. But Santa soon realized there was a limit to what he could do by himself. If he wanted to bring joy to tens or hundreds of millions of children, if he really wanted to cover the globe in a single night, he would need lieutenants. So he started hiring.

Unlike his elves, though, these new recruits would not work for candy canes. Sure, he could offer them new organs, weight reduction, life extension through hibernation and periodic injections, and other health benefits. We've gone over all that, and it certainly has proven to be a draw for prospective lieutenants. But from the start, Santa saw that it wouldn't be enough. Inevitably, the men wanted cash, too.

Generating enough money to reward his lieutenants after their five years of service—and finance those costly pre- and post-Christmas getaways—was not easy for Santa. I say Santa, but it's really Mrs. Claus who spearheads the business side of the outfit. Though we're often told she is quite a wizard with baked goods, in reality she's far more comfortable with a spreadsheet than a cookie sheet. (In the off-season she sometimes temps for a few months as an assistant at various Wall Street firms to pick up new trends. She has a wonderful freelance deal with the Swiss bank UBS.)

Mrs. Claus has given Santa a financial and management stake in a surprising number of technology-oriented Fortune 500 companies, but some of the first opportunities she identified were in old-world industries. For one, she essentially created the Christmas ornament business. This move was driven initially by aesthetics; she didn't like the fact that the living rooms her husband was visiting were filled with sparsely decorated trees, so she began designing ornaments herself. Initially she had Santa and his lieutenants deposit them for free in peoples' living rooms, but once ornaments became standard, and even desirable, she spearheaded the formation of a number of shadow companies to sell the tree trinkets on the open market. Manufacturing was never an issue; the ornaments self-assemble through a revolutionary, nature-inspired process explored in chapter 32.

Self-assembly has allowed her to keep these shadow companies streamlined, guaranteeing that the maximum possible profits funnel back to the Pole, but it also enables easy upgrades and add-ons. Toward the middle of the twentieth century, for example, Mrs. Claus ordered the addition of miniature listening devices, or bugs, to each of these ornaments. (This is the origin of the time-honored holiday warning "Quiet! My jingle bells are listening.") The change marked a significant upgrade to Santa's already robust surveillance network, which will be described in part 4. Let's just say he knows when—and where—you've been sleeping. And since his flying robots detect heat signatures, he can make a pretty good guess as to what you've been doing, too.

Mrs. Claus also recognized that Santa would need to maintain a relationship with the window and masonry businesses because of his reliance on wormhole-based time travel. This transportation system isn't foolproof. Santa's masonry and construction elves frequently have to upgrade and/or repair the time-travel equipment hidden in the windows and chimneys of the hundreds of millions of homes their boss and his lieutenants visit each year. Mrs. Claus realized that if their elves were going to be servicing these homes to begin with, and if they were forced to become experts in chimneys and windows so that they could retrofit them with the negative-energy generators needed to create the wormhole links between living rooms that enable Santa's lieutenants to quickly jump from house to house, well, then she might as well just take the next step and start a few companies. This way, they wouldn't have to be sneaky about getting access, and they'd generate extra revenue.

This is one of the reasons chimney-cleaning companies charge so much: A large portion of their fee goes to the North Pole. It also explains why the workers for such companies are so short and wear woolen caps in even the hottest weather. They're trying to hide their pointy little ears.

Not convinced? Consider this deft display of Clausian code work, which has eluded all but a few Harvard-trained symbologists. Mrs. Claus, it turns out, embedded a message in one of the first companies she formed as part of this new venture. If you rearrange the letters just so, "Anderson Windows" spells "Kris Kringle."

Okay, so maybe that's not true. Maybe you've got to switch some of the letters for new ones, too, and subtract a couple. But this doesn't make her strategy any less brilliant or original. In fact, these businesses are just a slice of Santa's empire.

Mrs. Claus also pushed for another route to easy wealth: She urged her husband to become a consultant. By the middle of the twentieth century, thanks in large part to the business development efforts of his wife, Santa Claus had built and cultivated advisory relationships with all of the major toy and leisure products companies, specialty goods manufacturers, retailers, and movie studios in the world. (He became friendly with numerous semioticians, too, but again, that was just for kicks. They make him giggle.) In the early years he would visit these clients on their own grounds, typically at night, when he could land his warp-drive-equipped sleigh on a company's roof without anyone noticing. But this extra travel eventually proved tiresome, and in 1957 he held the first of what would become an annual conference in Las Vegas.

Each year, typically during the first week of January, business leaders from a wide array of companies and industries pay enormous sums of money to listen to Santa and his lieutenants lecture on a variety of topics. They talk to executives in the home-design and -décor business about the evolving layout of living rooms; they honestly tell Pottery Barn designers how ridiculous those tables constructed from felled Argentinean cypress trees actually look in peoples' homes. They reveal charts displaying the historical growth of bust size in girls' dolls and, based on this information, project the ideal ratios for the following year. Linguists are brought in to uncover hidden desires in Christmas wish lists, and Santa's elves discuss new trends in supply-chain management. The little fellows actually tell Wal-Mart executives how to become more efficient, and they listen.

These lectures are open to all paying attendees; one-on-one meetings with the OC command an additional, much higher, fee. Apparently he gets even more than Bill Clinton.

On the Hollywood side, Santa presents anywhere from thirty to fifty screenplays. Though Santa, Mrs. Claus, and a few of his more creative elves often conceive the plots, his artificially intelligent robotic surgeons actually write the scripts. When they're not in the operating room, naturally. Many of these films are Christmas themed, and Santa often revises and adds to the works himself. But the robots also produce scripts in the action-adventure, romantic comedy, and horror genres. At the conference, studio executives bid for the rights, and Santa takes a percentage of the gross revenues if a movie is produced. This isn't a small business: Christmas films alone have earned several billion dollars at the box office, and Santa has taken home roughly 10 percent of that figure. As for other genres, I can't list specific films, but circumstantial evidence suggests that at least three of the top-ten grossing movies of 2008 were written by robots.

Employees of the Mandalay Bay hotel, the current site of this annual convention, might read these details and say, "Wait, I'm there every January, and I've never noticed two hundred old fat guys with white beards milling around with Bill Gates, Steven Spielberg, and other luminaries." But the truth is that you shouldn't notice, because all of the attendees and all of the presenters, including the OC himself, are required to impersonate Elvis Presley in costume, hairstyle, and diction. So, next time you overhear a pair of Elvis impersonators talking about whether kids prefer PCs or Macs, look again, to see just who it is that's hiding under that coiffure.

Though it is very much the focus, the Vegas meeting is not all business and marketing. It is also a chance for Santa and his lieutenants to unwind and relax after a physically and mentally grinding Christmas. Food, drink, long sessions of blackjack, massages, seaweed wraps: Santa sponsors everything his lieutenants desire. Except lap dances. That would just be wrong.

12

Memory-Erasing Milk

BRAIN PODS, LIEUTENANT RECRUITMENT, AND THE PUBLISHERS CLEARINGHOUSE SWEEPSTAKES

TOWARD THE END of the conference, Santa meets with each of his lieutenants individually. They review the year's performance over a cold glass of milk and some cookies, shake hands, and wish each other a happy new year. That is, unless the lieutenant's term happens to be expiring. If this is the case, they rarely make it to the handshake. Typically the lieutenant drops to the floor halfway through his milk.

No, Santa doesn't kill his ex-employees. He just knocks them out and erases their memories before returning them to their homes. These men do, after all, have lives to resume. The OC recruits them from all over the globe. Department-store Santas are always a good source; for all the deadbeats looking to make a few extra dollars off their extra pounds, there are some genuinely jolly, generous men working the malls. Santa also solicits doctors, entrenched public-school teachers, desk-bound newspaper reporters being pushed toward retirement because of the rise of Web-based journalism, leather goods salesmen, gnarly-knuckled locksmiths, and even the occasional information technology professional. The trade is irrelevant. What the OC looks for in his sub-Santas are qualities like joviality, generosity, and a high tolerance for repetition. What he wants is hardworking men who don't mind monotony.

Naturally there are other requirements. Fluency in foreign languages is a bonus, since Santa is a global figure. An ideal Santa is also at least fifty-five years of age, with a decent head full of hair. It doesn't necessarily have to be white: A little gene therapy turns the average new employee's locks to the hue of fresh snow in a matter of months.

Originally, he limited his search to large men, but since the obesity problem has become so significant, and Santa himself has shrunk his waistline, he now prefers skinnier lieutenants.

Most important, prospective Santas need to be willing to be away from their families for several years, and potentially (on the off chance they tunnel through a wormhole to an alternate universe) forever. If the prospective Santa is married, his wife has to give her blessing, which isn't an easy process, given that he can't tell her where he's going to be, or what he's going to be doing, for the next few years. He can only assure her that there won't be other women around and that he'll come back rich and, in all likelihood, far more healthy. Often this argument isn't sufficiently convincing; Santa has a much higher success rate with widowers and single men.

(You'd think he could get around the family problem by letting the employee work for him, then sending him back in time to a few minutes after he left for the North Pole in the first place, to carry on with life as usual. But the universe probably doesn't allow this kind of trickery, for reasons discussed in chapter 21. Besides, this would be terribly traumatic in the cases when lieutenants don't make it home.)

Now, how does Santa ensure that one of these lieutenants, after returning home, doesn't write a tell-all memoir describing his experiences? He erases their memories.

The science of how Santa trashes the files in his lieutenants' brains is a bit murky. It's also impossible to determine whether Santa uses this technology on Mrs. Claus, though it would obviously be advantageous if he were to engage in some sort of extramarital activity, in Las Vegas or elsewhere, and be caught in the act by his loving wife. What we do know is that contemporary research suggests that memory erasure, in general, doesn't look to be absolutely impossible. Yet it's not going to be easy to figure out, either—at least, not for scientists without the benefits of time travel and alien benefactors.

The first problem is that memories don't really have an address in the brain. You can't just fry a specific set of neurons and erase your recollection of the time you wet yourself in front of the entire elementary school during the finals of the spelling bee. You can't simply wipe out the bitterness of your victory, how what should have been one of your proudest days as a child turned out to be your worst.

That experience doesn't reside in a single tangle of neurons. Instead, scientists say that memories are stored diffusely, throughout the brain, and that they're constantly being maintained and refreshed.

Electroconvulsive therapy, or ECT, the process of delivering repeated jolts to the entire brain, has the capacity to wipe out several months' worth of mental files. Yet ECT doesn't really meet Santa's standards. For one, it's not entirely reliable. With ECT, memory erasure isn't a guarantee, so it's possible that a particularly crafty lieutenant, claiming to have no recollection of his Christmas duties following a shock, could then head back home and spill it all out in *People* a week later. Or he could craft a lengthy memoir, if it's the ex-journalist who emerges unaffected. Furthermore, if Santa or, in all likelihood, his robotic surgeons, had to repeatedly shock the lieutenants every few months, there's a strong chance he'd toast a brain now and then.

A drug called Halcion, commonly prescribed to treat insomnia, can cause memory loss, but this is an uncommon side effect, so, again, it wouldn't really be right for Santa. In both cases, ECT and Halcion, the technology has also been around for too long; Santa's highly advanced alien benefactors surely would have developed something much more efficient, even if their brains don't work quite like ours.

Today's basic research hints at such possibilities. In a 2006 experiment with lab rats, NYU neuroscientist Joseph LeDoux demonstrated that it's possible to soften traumatic memories, and the associated stress, without jamming up the rest of the brain. Another project, spearheaded by scientists at Israel's Weizmann Institute of Science, recently found that a peptide called ZIP can alter memories. ZIP halts the activity of an enzyme that some researchers think is key in maintaining long-term memories. In their study, which was coauthored by neuroscientist Todd Sacktor of the Downstate Medical Center of the State University of New York, the researchers trained lab rats to associate a specific scent with sickness. If water had this characteristic smell, the rats learned to avoid it. Once they were given ZIP, however, this association disappeared, and the rats resumed drinking the smelly water again.

This recent work might give us some clues to Santa's technique.

For instance, the milk and cookies. Why has Santa insisted that kids leave them out for all these years? Is he really that gluttonous? Or do the milk and cookies, and the fact that his lieutenants will naturally associate them with their deliveries, since they are one of the few common threads between the many living rooms they visit, somehow have a function in the deletion of their Christmas-related memories? Remember: They drink milk and eat cookies shortly before Santa knocks them out in Vegas. Is this the key? We don't know. It might only knock out the link, or association, and not the memory itself. There may be no hidden purpose here; it may be that Santa just really likes milk and cookies.

What we do know, getting back to the larger question of why anyone would want to sign on as a lieutenant, is that these men are returned home with no clue as to what they've just endured. Halfway through their glass of milk they tumble to the floor. A pair of elves rush in and wheel them out, and Santa calls in the next lieutenant. Meanwhile, the unconscious, mind-wiped former Santa is returned home.

There have been instances in which the sight of a Christmas tree, a gift that's wrapped just so, or even the taste of a candy cane has induced brief seizures in these former Santas, but no one has ever died from one of these reactions. Overall, in fact, they return home far healthier than when they left. They all get to keep their brain pods, for example. These MP3-player-sized devices, implanted under the scalp, constantly monitor an individual's mental health and administer small doses of drugs should they start tending toward depressive or compulsive states. (They also have a sleep-related function described in chapter 23.) With these and other upgrades, the men are all but guaranteed to be mentally and physically healthy for their last few decades on Earth.

Oh, and rich, too. This is critical, and, of course, it's the primary reason Santa and Mrs. Claus became so deeply involved in business in the first place. Santa needs to reward his workers. That said, a mysteriously fattened bank account wouldn't do. This would only spur confusion, trouble with the IRS, even perhaps a suspicion-ignited divorce if the men are married. Instead, after Santa returns him home, the standard ex-lieutenant, or his wife, answers the door the next day to discover that he has won the Publishers Clearinghouse sweepstakes. This often takes some convincing, as the men Santa recruits are generally fairly intelligent and suspicious of this very sketchy organization. But the money, they discover before long, is very real, and it allows the couple to retire happily.

13

The North Pole Is Melting

GLOBAL WARMING, ARCTIC ICE DEPLETION, AND THE PRECARIOUS POSITION OF SANTA'S HEADQUARTERS

ONCE THE CONFERENCE in Vegas wraps up and Santa erases the memories he needs to, he and his remaining lieutenants return to the North Pole. Not the literal North Pole, though, since that's really more of an idea than an actual place. It's merely a spot in the Arctic Ocean covered with sheets of ice one to three meters thick.

Unfortunately, the ice in this part of the world is disappearing. In the summer of 2008, the nineteen-square-mile Markham Ice Shelf split away, drifting off into the Arctic Ocean. Half of the Serson Ice Shelf, another enormous chunk of frozen water, did the same. One recent study predicts that the summertime covering of ice could be gone completely by 2040. This is an unsettling trend in terms of the health of the planet. Scientists with the National Oceanic and Atmospheric Administration, for example, are concerned that the loss of Arctic sea ice in the vicinity of the North Pole could change global ocean circulation. Water flowing in different directions might not sound like a big problem, but altering or weakening major ocean currents could damage marine life, put a serious chill on northern Europe, and dampen the sea's ability to suck greenhouse gases out of the air.

There's no doubt that this scenario is downright scary, but from Santa's perspective, it is far from the most immediate threat. Santa's aliens picked a location for his headquarters in northern Greenland. Presumably they chose it because it was remote, unpopulated, and dark through most of the winter months. It also afforded extra privacy, since the spot allowed them to situate the entire facility deep in a two-mile-thick sheet of ice. Apparently, though, these aliens do not have perfect foresight. They didn't anticipate that the Greenland ice sheet would start to melt.

Over the past several decades, climatologist Konrad Steffen has been studying the withering of this massive slab through a series of small observation stations. Thanks to his Greenland Climate Network, Steffen found that between 1992 and 2005, as global temperatures rose, the ice sheet dripped away at an increasing rate. Melting was a normal phenomenon in the warmer months, but from 1992 on, Steffen learned that it was taking place farther inland, and at higher altitudes, than ever before. A 2006 study that gathered data from a satellite observatory revealed that the sheet was shedding fifty-seven cubic miles' worth of ice per year. That's a seriously large ice cube, slightly less than four miles on a side. Just imagine the size of the cocktail that would include such voluminous chunks of ice, how long it would take to drink, and how hungover you'd be in the morning. Staggering.

Steffen believes that the Greenland Ice Sheet doesn't respond slowly to climate change, as conventional scientific wisdom would suggest. Instead, he thinks that water leaks down through fissures in the ice to the bedrock several miles below and actually accelerates the melting process. Other scientists have proposed that this rate will only increase as the years progress and that the melting of the Greenland Ice Sheet could be a major contributor to the rise of global sea levels in the coming decades. This wouldn't just raise the ocean's roof. All of that melted freshwater would also dilute the salination of the ocean and could alter major currents like the Gulf Stream.

This sort of development would be bad for a number of reasons—flooding low-lying coastal regions populated by millions of people, for example—but it's particularly jarring news for Santa. Surface melt has already dropped the height of the ice by several meters in some places on Greenland's sheet. As a result, the tops of several of Santa's buildings have become exposed and are at risk of being spotted by researchers like Steffen or even the thinning population of indigenous people. We can only hope that in either case, these witnesses will respect Santa's privacy and keep the secret to themselves. If not, though, he could always offer them a drug-laced glass of milk and wipe out their memories.

14

Living Green in Greenland

UNDERWATER TURBINES, SUPERCOOLED SERVER FARMS, AND AUTONOMOUS SUBMARINES

V ISITING VEGAS IS a difficult thing these days for environmentally concerned individuals. With its always-on bright lights and tremendous thirst, the city practically drains the blood from Mother Earth's veins. You'd think Santa and his crew would feel a bit guilty during their lengthy stay at this resource-swallowing oasis, but that's not really the case. They're immune to such feelings, given that they spend the rest of the year living in one of the greenest spots on the planet.

Various artists, writers, and filmmakers have painted Santa's workshop as anything from a series of quaint buildings to a small city crowded with stout, smoke-puffing brick factories. This is undoubtedly intentional; Santa, through his off-season film and creative work, clearly encourages this variety, so that no one will discover clues to the true nature and location of his headquarters. But the fact is that Santa's actual facilities would be difficult to depict from the outside. Until that ice started melting, they were entirely underground.

The Pole, as it's known to its residents, consists of living quarters for up to 300 lieutenants and more than 5,500 elves. The elves' rooms are typically half the size, in height and breadth, of those reserved for Santa and his lieutenants, so their wing is not much larger than a major Hilton. The Pole also has a small medical center, several chapels, numerous gymnasia and recreation facilities, and scattered cafeterias.

And what about the workrooms? Thanks to self-assembly, toys and other gifts are manufactured at the delivery point, in children's homes (see chapters 32 and 33), so there's no need for massive industrial plants staffed by assembly-line elves. There are a few workshops, but they're designed for engineering elves, not craftsmen. They serve as repair shops for the wormhole-based time machines and, on those rare occasions it's not running perfectly, Santa's warp-drive-powered sleigh. Most of the work at the Pole, though, is computer based.

The largest single room is a vast, cubicle-filled space packed with elves toiling away at advanced workstations. (The aliens, for those of you who are interested, use a Linux-like operating system.) Inside, they monitor the huge amounts of information piped in from Santa's widespread surveillance network, parsing data gathered by ornaments, satellites, and tiny, sensor-equipped flying robots. If you're trying to picture what this room looks like, imagine a crowded telemarketing center, then shrink all the workers and give them pointy little ears.

All of the data racing in, and all those computers, require servers, and these are housed in hundreds of thousands of square feet of climate-controlled rooms. Today, massive companies like Google and Microsoft work very hard to hide the number of servers they use because the machines are tremendous energy hogs. Since they need to be cooled constantly, they swallow up huge amounts of electricity. This is where that beneath-the-ice setting works to Santa's advantage and makes his alien benefactors look so brilliant. Santa's servers can't overheat; a series of fans suck in cold air from the icy surroundings, keeping the information technology heart of his operation constantly chilled.

Okay, so we've got numerous recreation centers. Several hotels' worth of living quarters. Thousands of computer workstations. A massive server farm. And yet the North Pole is green? How is that possible?

If you were to ask Santa that question, he'd smile awkwardly, try to laugh so that his no-longer-substantial belly shakes like a bowl full of jelly, and then hurry away, claiming that he has some urgent business to attend to. Why? Because he has no idea how most of this stuff works. He's good with gifts and people, but green technology? Not really his forté.

Ultimately, though, this doesn't matter, because the North Pole's power-generation infrastructure is entirely automated. Remember, Santa moved up there in the mid-nineteenth century. There were no televisions yet, let alone computers. If those aliens had tried to do a walk-through with old Jebediah Meserole, explaining all the technology at the Pole, plus how it's all powered, his head would have imploded. The guy was a shipbuilder. Yes, they handed him a stack of operations manuals, but they advised him not to open them. They told Santa it was all effectively magic, and that he wouldn't have to worry about a thing.

The Pole gets the majority of its power from a vast field of underwater turbines, the blades of which spin as ocean currents flow past. As in a wind turbine, the mechanical energy of the spinning blades is converted to electricity. This power is then routed to a central cable and carried back under the ice to the Pole. In places where the ocean's currents do not run so swiftly, underwater buoys that rise and fall as waves pass overhead generate additional power. The top of the buoys drop as a crest passes above them, then lift up as the trough of the wave flows by. From this simple up-down action, the buoy system borrows juice.

This alien technology is tremendously reliable, but the turbines are also serviced by autonomous underwater vehicles, or AUVs. When the performance of a particular turbine degrades, one of these Jet Ski–sized robotic submarines is dispatched to inspect the machinery. In recent years, companies like Chevron have funded the development of highly capable underwater robots in hopes that they could be used to service deep-sea oil wells. In some cases, future wells, which lie at the top of an oil pipe, may sit more than a mile below sea level, down at the very bottom of the ocean. Sending repairmen down wouldn't make sense, and accessing the wells via remote-controlled submarines would be too costly. Independent robotic submarines would be an ideal alternative, as they'd be able to inform engineers when or if real repairs are needed.

In Santa's system, the AUV navigates to its target using a form of sonar. It attaches itself to the turbine with a mechanical arm, then uses a series of scanners to check the surface of the machinery for dings, dents, or other flaws. With its manipulating arms and tools, the AUV can repair a range of defects itself, but in rare instances, when the needed work is beyond the robot's abilities, the faulty turbine is simply left to run until it degrades completely. A replacement self-assembles and comes online shortly thereafter.

The tragedy of Santa's green power system is that nobody knows about it. Alternative-energy companies pursuing the development of similar technologies down here in our alien-upgrade-free world would benefit hugely if people were aware of the fact that this technology really can work. A company called Verdant Power, for example, recently launched a pilot project in New York that hinged on underwater turbines. Initially, Verdant installed eight turbines in the river, and the devices did produce electricity. But the company also had a few setbacks—several turbine blades snapped in the river's strong currents, and skeptics said that the technology would never generate the kind of power promised. Now, if governments and investors only knew how many megawatts Santa draws from his turbines, and that he powers a small city primarily by borrowing energy from the ocean, they'd be only too happy to endure these little technological speed bumps and give Verdant and companies like it the funding they need to perfect their devices.

But don't blame Santa and Mrs. Claus. They're in the gift business. They don't have time to get involved with energy politics.

15

Why All Elves Are Clones

INDUSTRIOUS, RELATIVELY OBEDIENT, supremely resilient, and, best of all, small, elves are the ideal North Pole workers. They can live on only candy canes and water for weeks at a time. They don't have great entertainment needs; early Nora Roberts novels keep them happy. They require only a fraction of the living space of full-sized humans, and they love bunk beds. This is an added bonus, from a space-saving angle. At the Pole, five or six of them often live in a room no bigger than the average West Village studio apartment.

They don't complain about the food, the lack of natural light in the North Pole's underground dormitories, or the sixteen-hour days they spend staring at computer monitors, analyzing the data gathered by Santa's intelligence network (the specifics of which will be detailed in part 4). Yet there are still variations in their skill levels. Some elves are, quite simply, better at their job than others. And that's why they're allowed to reproduce only through cloning.

Let's step back a bit. The elf population started small, with fifty-seven pointy-eared individuals reporting for the first year's work. (We don't know where they came from; it may be that they are aliens themselves. Vulcans, perhaps. Mr. Allen, would you care to respond?) In the beginning, though, Santa's operation was also relatively tiny. That number of elves was totally sufficient. When he began hiring lieutenants, though, and slowly expanded his reach across the globe, the number of children he had to keep an eye on throughout the year expanded, too. The flow of surveillance data became too great for fifty-seven elves to manage.

The engineering work increased exponentially, too. More homes to visit meant more wormhole time machines to install and maintain. Thankfully, though, Santa's operation was designed to be scalable. Santa's aliens predicted growth and built in a computerized management system that expands the elfish population in anticipation of increased workflow.

Each elf is constantly rated and ranked in terms of productivity and efficiency, and only the top workers are cloned. If the system estimates that Santa's operation will require, say, ten new workers a year for a given period, in a given discipline, then ten clones of the year's most efficient elf in that area will be created. They won't be ready to work right away, though. There's no growth acceleration technique, as in the cloning films *The Island* and *The Sixth Day*, so there is a waiting period. That said, child labor laws do not apply at the North Pole, so elf kids can start working as early as age nine.

Is this eugenics-style approach deplorable? Absolutely. Morally vacuous? Without a doubt. Yet we must not blame Santa himself, as he is completely unaware of how it works. He only knows that he always has the right number of capable, efficient workers every year. The aliens did it, so if you wish to protest, direct your outrage at the cosmos. And do so at night, since it will be hard for them to notice you during the day, because the sun gets in the way. If you're going to use signs, they should probably be really big. And well lit.

Contemporary scientists have adopted a similar approach to cloning canines. In early 2008, the Korea Customs Service announced that it had commissioned a group of scientists to clone an accomplished drug-sniffing dog, to test whether the technique would produce better crime busters. In the end, three different surrogate mothers gave birth to a total of seven cloned puppies. When these clones were put through a series of tests designed to determine a dog's potential fitness as a drug detector, all seven of them passed. In comparison, eight normal dogs took the test, and only one of them was identified as a potential candidate.

The dog doubles were produced via the most popular cloning technique, known as somatic cell nuclear transfer. On a surface level this method seems pretty simple. Take a female egg; remove its genetic material. Next, pull the nucleus out of a cell derived from the dog, or elf, to be cloned, and pop that into the egg. Then cultivate the combination in the lab until it's a viable embryo. Finally, when everything looks good and healthy, implant it into the womb of an adult female of the same species. See? Easy as 1-2-3. And from that point, Mother Nature takes over.

But it doesn't always work. The group that produced those drug-sniffing dogs previously turned out the world's first canine clone, but they burned through 1,095 embryos along the way. They implanted embryos in 123 surrogate mothers but produced only three pregnancies and a single success. The scientists did witness two births, but one of the pups died after just twenty-two days.

The specifics aren't available in this case, but if we assume that the North Pole uses a similar though more efficient cloning technique, then it would be a fairly simple setup, and one that neither Santa nor his elves would even need to be cognizant of. The male elves would have to be sterilized at birth, and it's likely that representatives of both genders would be forced to take and adhere to a vow of celibacy. Santa needs them to be resting in their off-hours, not jumping from bunk to bunk. Which makes you wonder why he allows them to read so many Nora Roberts novels. But that's another matter; elfish sexual behavior is a topic for a different book.

Santa's robotic surgeons could remove and store sample cells from each elf and maintain a supply of eggs removed from female elves. This way, they'd be able to initiate cloning when prompted by the population-management software. Healthy embryos would likely be cultivated in artificial wombs, since popping them into supposedly celibate lady elves would surely stir up some controversy and, in turn, have a negative effect on productivity. (Undoubtedly the elves would suspect Santa, since all the males are sterilized and the big chief has been caught staring at the little ladies on occasion.)

Post-birth, the cloned elf children would be reared like normal kids. Sure, growing up trapped inside an underground facility, destined to become a constantly monitored drone chained to a computer at the age of nine, might not sound like a normal childhood. But remember: They get candy canes. As many as they want.

PART IV

Surveillance

16

Kringle's Eyes in the Skies

UNMANNED AERIAL VEHICLES, MINIATURE FLYING ROBOTS, AND WHY THE CHRISTMAS ALIENS MAY HAVE UNWITTINGLY ADVANCED MILITARY SURVEILLANCE

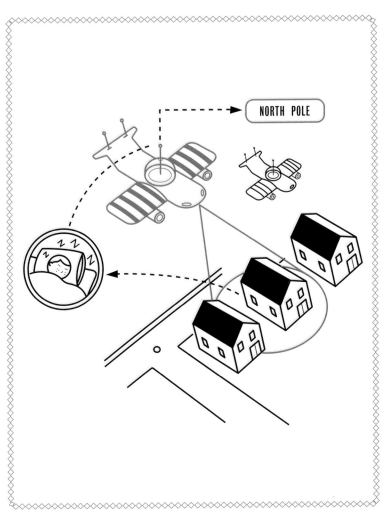

NORTH POLE

DECEMBER TWENTY-THIRD. SANTA'S lieutenants are well rested and ready for another round of deliveries, thanks to their annual pre-Christmas stay in Hawaii. A few too many chilled, golden Kona Longboard Lagers and some extra time in the sun haven't hurt; a little redness in the face and an extra inch or two around the waist enhance a lieutenant's Kringle-ness.

Santa and Mrs. Claus are refreshed, too. The elves have been working hard, as usual, but the onset of the holiday season gives them an added burst. They no longer mind the hours, the glow of their OLED screens, the repetitive stress injuries.

But what have they been doing while Santa and his crew relaxed? Not manufacturing toys, as we've all been taught to believe. Nearly every gift Santa delivers assembles itself, on-site, from a collection of micro- and nano-scale components (see chapter 32). Yes, there is maintenance work. Wormhole-based time machines require frequent tuning and need to be resupplied with fuel to generate the necessary amounts of negative energy, the stuff that actually keeps the wormholes open. A sizable population of elves stays busy fixing chimneys and windows and conducting tests to ensure that the surveillance equipment Santa has deployed over the years is all still working properly.

Generally, though, the period from February through mid-December is focused on intelligence gathering. Santa taps into phone conversations, e-mails, text messages, and more. On occasion, he takes advantage of the highly sensitive listening devices embedded in many Christmas ornaments. These "bugs" can pick up arguments in the basement even when the decorative trinkets themselves are tucked away in a box in the attic. They can identify a back-talking child from a hundred feet.

But Santa is very much from the actions-speak-louder-than-words school of morality, so he's far more interested in what children do than what they say or write. He believes it's more important to monitor their actions than their speech, so most of his surveillance efforts are focused on video. And although he does tap into security cameras in schools, malls, and, if they're digital, even homes, he captures most of his data independently, with the help of an enormous fleet of unmanned aerial vehicles, or UAVs. In less technical terms: Santa's got flying robot spies.

In the non-Christmas world, UAVs monitor borders for illegal crossings, scope out battlefields, and drop bombs. The military's Predator UAV can identify the heat signature of a person from ten thousand feet. And although the people who develop these robots like to comfort themselves by pointing out how they can be used for good causes like studying the atmosphere and helping scientists better understand the spread of aerial pollution and other large-scale climate-related phenomena, UAVs are basically war machines.

Santa has no use for bombs or missiles, but surveillance is absolutely critical. Throughout the year, a fleet of Santa's flying robots constantly canvases suburban and rural neighborhoods. They sweep a predesignated grid, coasting back and forth across a zone that typically covers one or two towns, constantly recording video.

Now, I know what you're thinking: How would Santa use a high-flying UAV to monitor a city? Given the height of the buildings, the numerous crisscrossing streets, and the density, is there any way one or even a few of these flying robots could perform effectively from thousands of feet up? That's a good question. But it's kind of irrelevant, given that Santa doesn't use the usual flying robots to spy on urban environments. Instead, he deploys millions of mosquito- and dragonfly-sized micro aerial vehicles, or MAVs.

These tiny mechanical flying insects peer down alleyways and into elevators and apartments, darkened bars, and exclusive restaurants. Capable of capturing simple pictures or identifying heat signatures that indicate the presence of humans, the robotic flies provide Santa with a comprehensive picture of who is sleeping and who is awake, and, when used in conjunction with other surveillance gear, they can provide him with the data necessary to pick out specific actions or encounters.

While I'd like to reassure you here that this technology would never, ever be used for anything other than the safe, accurate, and speedy delivery of presents, this may not actually be the case. Numerous rumors have surfaced suggesting that the U.S. government has been using tiny, flying surveillance robots to spy on political gatherings and public protests. Given the status of today's technology, this seems totally ridiculous and conspiratorial. There are MAVs small enough to fit on the tip of your pinkie finger, and at least one of them actually does fly. But, as of 2008, this particular mechanical marvel had to be attached to a set of guide wires. It also sucked its energy through a tether connected to an external power source. One leading expert in the field has said that he doesn't expect truly autonomous MAVs to be flying in the lab for at least another five years. Interestingly, he also asked that his name not be included in this book, which strongly suggests that he has ties to Santa Claus, or at least believes in him, and worries that divulging too many technical details could decrease his Christmas-morning haul.

The point, though, is that today's MAVs sure don't sound ready to hover over political events, collecting data on protestors. Yet we know that Santa's robots could. And based on the incredibly small size of his MAVs, we can assume that they won't always make it back to the North Pole. Occasionally they'll make a mistake, confuse a closed window for an open passageway, slam into the glass, and fall apart. They might even look appetizing to a hungry bird and end up in the gut of a sparrow.

This suggests the possibility that at some point in the past, government researchers collected a few broken, left-behind models of Santa's MAVs and reverse-engineered them, creating miniature drones of their own. And that they are now using their alien-tech-based creations to spy on us. So, pull your shades, lower your voice, and find yourself a heavy-duty fly swatter.

17

Naughty or Nice

S ANTA'S ELVES ARE diligent analysts, but even they would find it impossible to scour all the video recorded by his surveillance drones in addition to the material swiped from security and home cameras. Those clips do need to be examined, but the elves couldn't review them all. Thankfully, Santa's video analytics software picks out the highlights.

Today, this technology is poised to revamp the security industry. Think about that classic movie scene of the single underpaid guard watching a bank of screens for hours at a time. The heroes, or villains, always dupe that poor, doughnut-stuffed soul. But what if it wasn't his job to search for threats? What if a computer did the scanning for him and only asked him to weigh in on real problems?

In the last few years, companies have begun turning out software programs that can search through video for figures who are lingering too long in one place, unattended packages, or even trespassers hopping a fence or wall. A company called Vidient, for example, has developed a technology called SmartCatch that automatically detects suspicious action at airports, warehouses, and other locations. Smart-Catch is also being used in schools to watch for people hanging around too long where kids are being dropped off. The computers and cameras do all the work, so the security guards don't turn brain-dead staring at their screens and miss that suspicious loiterer. The software decides what's important enough to pass back to security or school officials. These people can then choose how to respond.

This software could soon become far more intelligent. In 2004, while conducting his Ph.D. research at the University of Texas–Austin, computer-vision specialist Sangho Park described a system that could track individuals and gauge their behavior toward one another as neutral, aggressive, or friendly. His program, which is still under development, would analyze each image in a video stream and effectively frame different people and their associated body parts—arms, legs, etc. After distinguishing each person, the program would monitor how he or she acts relative to others in the scene. So, if two arms are linked but attached to different bodies and moving in an up-down motion from one frame to the next, this might register as neutral or friendly behavior. The two people are probably shaking hands. But if one of these arms is moving quickly toward and away from the other body, or frame, this could be a sign of aggression. That person could be pushing or punching the other.

The key step forward here is that a system of this kind wouldn't just track the motion of individuals. It would try to interpret the meaning of the motion.

Santa's video analytics program is fairly similar, though far more robust. With the footage gathered by digital school video cameras and flying robots, his software can easily find bullies, but it also catches kids who are cutting class, passing notes, stealing the Fruit Roll-Ups from a classmate's lunch box, cheating on tests, and more. His pointy-eared analysts, therefore, aren't tasked with sifting through infinite hours of useless footage. They're only asked to make high-level decisions. The software sends them just the important video clips, and, by reviewing them, the elves quickly confirm or deny the conclusion reached by the program itself.

Yet video analytics has its limits and will probably never be Santa's primary way of figuring out who has been naughty and who has been nice. Instead, Santa hones in on one of the most powerful forces in the universe.

Guilt.

18

Guilt-Ridden Visions of Sugarplums

WHY REMOTE EEG DETECTION PROVIDES SANTA WITH A MORE ACCURATE DETERMINATION OF BEHAVIOR

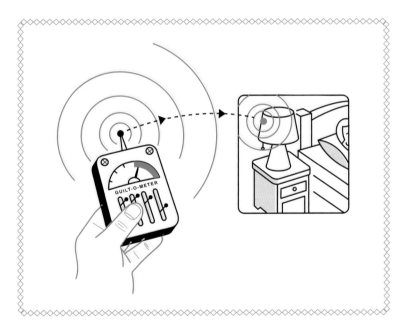

THE ALIENS MUST have known about the strong correlation between Christianity and guilt (who doesn't?) because Santa's system capitalizes on the link. Somewhere in each child's room, typically in a lamp or other light fixture, but probably in bedside tables, too, since Santa has long had ties to the home furnishings industry, there is a remote electroencephalogram (EEG) detector.

These devices measure the brain's electrical activity; conspiracy theorists suspect that they're linked to something called remote neural monitoring. They believe that the U.S. National Security Agency can detect all of our thoughts, even over large distances. Today's researchers profess that this is all but impossible, or at least far out of the reach of modern technology. Not convinced? Try this simple experiment. Look up the name of the current director of the National Security Agency, and picture him or her in a clown suit, then a bikini. Now imagine his wife in the nude. If you are not arrested on suspicious charges within twenty-four hours, or, if you are a woman and he does not contact you and suggest that you, he, and his wife get together and try on some circus costumes, it should be clear to you that remote neural monitoring is not possible.

Still, this stuff isn't all science fiction. Scientists have shown that they can pick up brain waves remotely. A group at the University of Sussex in the UK demonstrated that they can read electroencephalograms from more than ten feet away. These brain waves don't give away your thoughts, but scientists have been able to associate different EEG frequencies with specific emotions and cognitive states. So, they can generally link certain EEG readings to feelings like anger, joy, sorrow, and relaxation.

The Sussex remote-detection technology, though far too large to store in a bedside table or lamp, is the closest in nature to Santa's system. Rather than pick out particular memories or thoughts, Santa's EEG detectors scan for guilt and remorse, which often intensify as Christmas approaches and children begin to wonder if they've been good enough during the year. In bed at the end of each day, as the kids mentally review their bad deeds, their guilt readings spike. If a child's levels continue to grow as the big day approaches and exceed a specific, predetermined guilt threshold, that child is flagged. And if a particular child shows no remorse whatsoever, he or she is assumed to be particularly devilish.

This is where the video highlights come into play. The elves have a file on each child; they can review them when necessary and then continue to monitor them, compiling more evidence through standard surveillance, including listening devices, satellites, and flying robots.

And then? If proven guilty, does little Billy get a nice, dusty, lung-wrecking bag of coal to teach him to stop spitting in his classmates' lunches when they're not looking? No. The continued association of Santa with coal has been a colossal mistake, for various reasons.

It not only reflects poorly on Santa's environmental awareness; it also creates some troubling questions about Santa's understanding of child psychology. The truth is that Santa has shifted away from punishment entirely. Thanks to Mrs. Claus, he now practices positive reinforcement.

19

Why Santa Ditched Coal

THE PSYCHOLOGY OF POSITIVE REINFORCEMENT, ADOLESCENT BEHAVIOR, AND A REGRETTABLE PENCHANT FOR UNJUSTIFIED SPANKINGS

IN THE EARLY days, when Santa's operations were confined to Christian homes in the U.S., the task of determining, based on the evidence gathered via surveillance and guilt monitoring, whether a given child was naughty or nice was relatively simple. Behavior was measured against a standard code: the Ten Commandments. Generally, the worthiness of a child would be determined by how closely he or she hewed to the rules of the Christian faith. But then Christmas spread across the globe and across interfaith lines. And for many children, it had more to do with getting new bicycles than trying not to covet their neighbors' rides.

As a result, some of Santa's most influential elves and lieutenants began arguing that the behavior of children should be judged according to the standards of their own religion or culture. Santa detested this idea, dismissing his critics as moral relativists. Santa believed in the Ten Commandments and felt everyone else should, too.

This seemed like a critical issue, and one that would only become more important as Santa's reach expanded, but eventually Mrs. Claus proved that it was actually irrelevant. Citing several new trends in child psychology, she demonstrated that the standards question was not as crucial as it appeared. In the 1960s and '70s, she began making Santa aware of a kind of paradigm shift among child and family psychologists. "Here's a fresh plate of cookies, dear," she'd say, "and a very intriguing new paper from a group at Yale." She stacked his bedside table with research and the complete works of the Harvard child psychologist Robert Coles.

The gist of this growing body of research was that the kind of negative reinforcement that Santa practiced by filling the stockings of naughty children with coal was useless. It wasn't just mean. It was ineffective. Positive reinforcement was proving to be far more powerful when it came to altering a child's behavior. Today this approach is accepted knowledge and has been backed up by numerous studies.

Yet it took a while for Mrs. Claus to change Santa's thinking on the subject. He remained doubtful in part because all of this research hasn't necessarily translated into a healthy crop of youngsters. Psychologists have found that children are more anxious and depressed today than ever before. And not just poor or downtrodden kids, or bullies who live in busted or abusive homes. The mental backpacks of wealthy children are also stuffed with psychological issues. A recent Columbia University study, for example, cited the fact that upperclass children can be more susceptible to depression, anxiety, and substance abuse.

Santa was also just plain fond of the coal punishment. He liked giving nasty little kids a few chunks of the stuff and imagining how the punks felt when they saw their stockings in the morning. He enjoyed a bit of casual corporal punishment, too. In the 1960s, he was prone to spanking his elves after drinking too greedily from Mrs. Claus's famously large bowls of eggnog. But the evidence for positive reinforcement was irrefutable, and the elves threatened revolt if the spankings continued, so Santa was eventually forced to adapt.

These days, instead of punishing children for immoral or unfriendly actions, Santa rewards them for good deeds. When guilt levels picked up by the remote EEG detector fall within the standard or normal range, a note is attached to a child's wished-for gift that compliments him on his good behavior. If guilt levels are too high or, for reasons explained earlier, suspiciously low, then Santa's analytics software mines the video captured by school and other security cameras, plus his own flying drones, for examples of good behavior. It picks out nefarious acts, too, in order to confirm that the child has actually acted poorly and isn't merely subject to a heightened sense of guilt that makes him feel as though even the smallest slight directed at another child is equivalent to a mortal sin. The real point, though, is to identify not those instances in which the bully stole a lunch or tripped an unsuspecting book hound, but instead those when he happened to help another child. Here again, a note is attached: "This is for giving little Timmy Hartwell a hand when he stumbled in gym class."

It is still too early to measure the effect of Santa's tactical shift on the larger population, too premature to see whether he has helped diminish those anxiety and depression numbers through his mission, but one thing is clear: The elves are thrilled that he stopped the spankings.

PART V

Transportation

20

The Chimney as Wormhole Mouth

HOW SANTA'S HELPERS VISIT ALL THOSE HOMES IN A SINGLE NIGHT

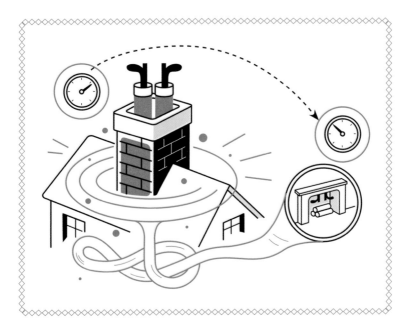

CHRISTMAS EVE AT the Pole begins with a long, luxurious meal. When the eggnog is served, the OC stands before his lieutenants and delivers a stirring speech about the importance of Christmas, the joy each man will spread through his work, how all their toil will help make the world a better place. Much cheering and singing follow, until the Santas are cut off from the alcohol and served strong coffee brewed from freshly roasted and ground organic beans, often from Yemen. (The aliens must be coffee snobs, too, because the Pole is scattered with numerous top-quality cafés.)

Then the mood shifts. Revelry gives way to focus. Each lieutenant confers with his elfish handlers, reviewing their plans. If the Santas are astronauts, these elves, back at their workstations, constitute NASA's mission control. They track the lieutenants throughout the night.

Finally, at midnight, Eastern Standard Time (because the OC is from Brooklyn, after all), each Santa grabs his sack full of equipment, throws it over his shoulder, walks to his designated departure portal, and dives through.

I know what you're thinking. A departure portal? No sleigh? No, not for the lieutenants. So how do they pay all those visits in a single night without a vehicle? In the 1994 remake of *Miracle on 34th Street*, Sir Richard Attenborough's Santa character suggests that he accomplishes the seemingly impossible by slowing time down. This isn't completely off base. Time can flow at different speeds. Near the event horizon of a black hole, for example. The gravitational pull there is so great that time itself gets stretched. Someone resilient enough to survive near the edge of one of these matter-devouring cosmic beasts would age more slowly than someone sitting back on Earth. The same goes for someone moving at an incredibly fast pace. Einstein showed that the closer you get to the speed of light, the more time slows down relative to someone who remains stationary.

But for Santa to make this work, he would have to either pop all of humanity into a light-speed-fast spaceship while he and his lieutenants completed their rounds, or increase the gravitational pull in and around peoples' homes enough that the added force would stretch seconds into hours. The downside of this tactic, though, is that it would probably cause the homes and all their occupants to implode. Merry Christmas! You've been gravitationally squashed down to the size of a tick!

Aha, but what if Santa sped up? What if he pulled an impersonation of the Flash and raced around the world at light speed? If he were to move that fast, according to Einstein's ideas, time would flow much more slowly for him than for those sleeping kids. His body's clock would slow down. Every motion would take a little bit longer. So, even if he could travel from point A to point B in an instant, he wouldn't actually be able to get much done en route. Wrapping a simple gift would take him forever if he was moving at that speed. So this is not an option.

No, Santa and his lieutenants always move at a generally human pace. Even if they're hopped up on performance enhancers, it's going to take them roughly thirty seconds to scope out a living room, run through their routine, and then exit. And he uses those lieutenants because it would take roughly 190 years, without travel time, for a single Santa to drop off presents in two hundred million homes.

But we've already gone over some of these details. This is the whole reason Santa has lieutenants and doesn't do the job himself. Yet even when that workload is divided among hundreds of people, it still takes a while. In fact, each Santa spends slightly more than six months delivering presents on Christmas Eve.

Now, that's six months of their time, of course. To us, only a night passes. To complete all that work before the first kids wake up, hoping to get a glimpse under the tree, the Santas have to time-travel. It's absolutely essential. As they move from house to house, they move from one spot in space to another, but they also shift from one point in time to another.

So, how do they manage this feat? There are some things we still don't know, but it is fairly clear that the mode of transport/time-travel they use is based on astrophysical oddities called wormholes. These strange passageways consist of three basic parts: two mouths, one of which is an entrance, the other an exit, and a tunnel, or throat, that connects them. Wormholes may be able to link distant, or even not-so-distant, parts of the universe via relatively short paths. Scientists think they might offer shortcuts through space and time.

The idea that the universe might allow for something like a wormhole was first proposed by Einstein and a pair of collaborators, but its potential use as a time machine wasn't explored in any real detail until Caltech astrophysicist Kip Thorne decided to devote some brain power to the topic. In 1988, by managing to get their first paper on the subject published in a prestigious journal, *Physical Review Letters*, Thorne and his colleagues effectively legitimized wormholes as a topic for serious thinkers.

One of the common ways of explaining how wormholes work involves a sheet of paper. Imagine this paper represents our entire universe. On one end, mark point A; on the far side, point B. Now let's say that you are a little dot on that paper, a citizen of this tremendously thin world. You're at a party at point A, but you're a little bored, and your friend texts you about a much cooler gathering at point B. One with celebrities. Unfortunately, this second party is getting crowded, so you need to get there soon, before the hosts close the doors. If this paper universe is lying flat, then the shortest distance between A and B is a straight line. You just need to start running.

But if this paper world happens to be folded over so that points A and B are nearly touching, and you happen to be aware of the fact that your universe, this piece of paper, is actually floating in a higher-dimensional plane that allows it to be bent, folded, dropped, or transformed into an airplane, then you have another option. There is a shorter path. Forget sticking to the paper; you could move through that higher space. If you could punch two holes in the paper, one next to A and the other next to B, and then find a drinking straw that slips into those two gaps, you wouldn't have to travel all that way across the paper, around the fold. You could just slip through the straw, like a slide, and get to the party in a fraction of the time.

The straw, in this case, is the wormhole. These tunnels, by dipping into a different kind of space, offer shortcuts through space-time. Does that make sense? No? Fine; forget the paper. Imagine that first party is in a third-story apartment. The other one is downstairs, right below it. Convention suggests that the only way to get from one apartment to the other is to exit through the door, descend the stairs, and head down the hall to the second apartment. In the wormhole version, though, you'd get a jackhammer, bust a hole through the floor, drop right down into the other apartment, and grab yourself a drink.

Still no? Okay, take that piece of paper again, flatten it out, and make those two holes large enough for your hands to fit through, but not so big that you end up ripping the paper. Carefully stick each hand through, and extend them out in front of you. This might not help you understand wormholes, but now you know what it's like to be a painter in a post-canvas art world, handcuffed to a dying medium.

The truth is that the paper example, which normally doesn't involve drinking straws or parties, is one of those tricky analogies that make people feel like they understand a concept even though they really don't. It offers a two-to-three-dimensional example of what is really a three-to-four-dimensional phenomenon. We're better off admitting that we can't fully visualize these things and going from there. Wormholes equal shortcuts through space and time. Good. Let's move on.

Picturing wormholes may be difficult, but it's easy to imagine their effects. Let's say your front door is one wormhole mouth and the other is located at your neighbor's front door. Your doorbell rings. You open the door, and there's a singing telegram outside. The courier is kind of funny looking, but she appears to be trustworthy, and it's your birthday, too, so you invite her in. When she steps forward through the door frame and into the mouth of the wormhole, however, she disappears.

If the tunnel between the two mouths is short—say, a foot in length—she'll immediately reemerge from your neighbor's front door and step into his foyer instead of your own. (That is, assuming you both have foyers.) What would happen next depends on whether you and your neighbor have the same birthday, and whether he or she has a history of drug use and/or marital infidelity, but you get the point. The telegram singer walks into one home and finds herself in a completely different one.

There have been advances in the research since Thorne and his colleagues first published their paper, but wormholes are not going to put the airlines out of business anytime soon. Constructing one, holding the two mouths open, and putting everything together in such a way that a person, or a spaceship, could travel through the tunnel to the other end without having every molecule in their body torn apart is really, really difficult.

Yet scientists continue to study the idea. Francisco Lobo of the University of Lisbon, in Portugal, has suggested in a number of recent papers that new work in astrophysics may provide a clue to the potential workings of wormholes. In the last decade or so, astronomers have become increasingly convinced that the universe is expanding under the pressure of a mysterious force. This so-called dark energy acts as a kind of antigravity, pushing the cosmos apart while gravity works to pull all those planets, stars, and galaxies closer together. How does it work? Nobody's quite sure yet, which is why they call it "dark" energy. That's code for "we don't know."

One of the biggest perceived difficulties with wormholes is keeping the mouths—the entrances and exits—to the tunnels from closing up. Gravity collapses things, so, to build a working wormhole, you'd need something to counteract that inward pull. One physicist has suggested that you would need the negative-energy equivalent of a Jupiter-sized chunk of mass to prevent a mouth just one meter wide from closing. That's the mass of roughly 318 Earths converted into energy. So, you know, it would be really hard to do.

Lobo suggests that a version of the dark energy astrophysicists have been buzzing about, called phantom energy, might also prove effective. The same stuff that's pushing the cosmos apart could counteract gravity and keep the mouth wide open. Lobo writes that recent theoretical work on phantom energy has "far-reaching physical and cosmological implications, namely, apart from being used for interstellar shortcuts, an absurdly advanced civilization may convert [wormholes] into time machines."

In his original paper, Thorne suggests that an "infinitely advanced civilization" might be able to make this work. Lobo talks about an "absurdly advanced civilization." None of these papers mention Santa explicitly, but this can probably be attributed to the fact that the scientists don't know about the aliens, who have absurdity and advancement in large quantities.

They are also incredible planners. The transit system they established for Santa's operations was designed to be scaled up along with the rest of his operation, and it works primarily through chimneys and windows. The average home is connected, via wormhole, to two other homes. In other words, each house has an "entrance" and an "exit" mouth. Typically, the former is located in the living room window and the latter in the fireplace or within the frame of a painting. (Honestly, has anyone ever really seen him enter through a chimney? No.) If one of Santa's lieutenants wants to exit a home, he simply jumps through the wormhole mouth in the fireplace or the frame. A moment later he pops out of a window at his next destination.

In a way, this system defies some of the logic inherent in modern wormhole research, which typically suggests that these strange tunnels would be most useful in facilitating astronomical shortcuts, or hops from one galaxy to another instead of one home to another. This apparent contradiction shouldn't lead us to suspect that Santa is trying to mislead us, though. Instead, we should think of it as yet another testament to the brilliance of his alien benefactors. They are so far beyond us in their understanding of the universe that the equations our theorists diddle with today must look as simplistic as cave paintings to them.

Also, the house-to-house link isn't true in every case. Some homes are linked back to the North Pole—otherwise Santa wouldn't be able to begin his journey by diving through that first portal—and others join up with warehouses, for reasons to be explained in chapter 32.

This transit system has proven to be tremendously effective, but by the late 1990s, Santa was actually approaching the upper limit on the number of homes his lieutenants could visit via wormhole, due to the phenomenal energy requirements. Santa only has a finite amount of energy available each year, and he was nearly exhausting it to keep all those wormhole mouths from collapsing under the pressure of gravity. Coincidentally, his waistline mandate has removed this cap for the foreseeable future. The average diameter of a lieutenant's waist has shrunk considerably, which means that the wormhole mouths don't need to be as wide, either. (The lieutenants all dive in headfirst.) And because the mouths are smaller, the amount of negative energy each one burns is smaller, too. So, skinnier Santas are better in more ways than one.

The true beauty of Santa's wormhole-based travel technique, though, is that it enables his lieutenants to recover the time they lose dropping off gifts in a given house. Each wormhole deposits a lieutenant in the next living room on his schedule a few hundredths or tenths of a second after he arrived in the previous one. As a result, at any moment, a given lieutenant may actually be working in thousands of different homes at once. By the time he visits three houses, roughly ninety seconds have elapsed for him, but because he time-travels, a mere fraction of a second has passed on Earth.

Wormholes may be an effective means of cramming nearly a year's worth of work into the span of a few hours, but they're not perfect. They are extremely dangerous, and sometimes unstable. This is one of the reasons the OC rewards his lieutenants so generously, and it's also why he refuses to travel via wormhole himself, relying instead on a warp-drive-enhanced sleigh.

The OC loses one Santa to a wormhole-related accident, on average, every other Christmas. This is far worse than the mortality rates for commercial fishing, mining, and truck driving, three of America's most dangerous jobs. And these wormhole glitches offer a death that's just as frightening as falling over the side of a boat into the frigid sea or slowly asphyxiating in a partially collapsed mine. A mismanaged or malfunctioning throat can send a person to an alternate and considerably less jolly universe, crush him like a steamroller flattening a grasshopper, or hit him with so much radiation that his cells fry like eggs. (This might explain why Santa and his lieutenants drink so much nog. It may not be a celebratory drink at all, but a crutch that helps them dull the painful memories of lost comrades.)

Sometimes these breakdowns are the result of simple mechanical malfunctions, but on occasion, prying children may be at fault. That's right, kids: You can kill Santa Claus.

A Few Brief Thoughts About the Effects of Time Travel on Book Reading

At this point you might be thinking that you should skip the next chapter because, based on the logic of the last one, you've already read it. And if you have any sort of confidence in yourself, you're probably assuming that you understood the ideas expressed therein, too.

This is a totally reasonable assumption. After all, the lieutenants' time-traveling, their whole process of moving forward and then backward in time as they visit all those homes, suggests that the past, present, and future all coexist. They're simultaneous. In other words, the future has already happened. We don't need to bother reading difficult chapters because we've already read and, presumably, taken the time to understand them, in the future.

So, honestly, what did you think? No, don't answer that.

The fact is that even if this were the case, which isn't clear, then one could argue that the coexistence of the past/present/future should actually strengthen your resolve as a reader. By lazily refusing to absorb the next chapter on the grounds that you've already read it at some point a few minutes or hours or weeks from now, you'll risk unalterably changing that future. This seemingly harmless act could change the course of your life, or someone else's, forever. You could prevent the Chicago Cubs from winning the World Series or force your unborn grandchild to one day flunk a critical entrance exam. And if that were the case, Santa definitely wouldn't bring you any presents.

Thankfully, there is also another option. If, in reading this book, you have acquired enough knowledge about the universe to construct your own time machine, then you could, after reading the next chapter, use that time machine to unread it. This would be much more tolerable, morally, than refusing to read.

Ideally, you would travel back to the moment you began reading this chapter, stop yourself, maybe pour a refreshing drink, and skip ahead to chapter 22. This is assuming, of course, that you didn't put down the book for a few hours, days, or weeks because of this chapter. If that's the case, you should just try to forget the experience and forgo the time traveling. Now that you have a time machine, you should know that it's very important to avoid canceling or reliving large chunks of your life because of a few paragraphs of text. A few minutes, sure. But no more.

21

How to Kill a Santa

CHRISTMAS EVE, TIME TRAVEL, AND
THE TROUBLE WITH CAUSALITY

EVERY SANTA-LOVING CHILD is told to refrain from sneaking out in the middle of the night to take a look under the tree, but parents rarely explain why this is such a problem. Which is totally understandable. Most seven-year-olds don't take to lectures on causality.

Berkeley astrophysicist Richard Muller thinks that Santa's refusal to drop off presents for kids who catch a midnight glimpse of the tree may not just be principle. The thing about time travel is that it would very likely come with a few rules. For instance, some scientists have suggested that the universe will only permit time travel if it doesn't interfere with causality. With regards to Santa, Muller says this translates to: "He can't change events that have already happened."

Generally, time-travel paradoxes are framed in terms of dramatic actions. Going back in time and killing your father before you were conceived, for example. The implications of that one are brain-crushingly difficult to ponder. But causality probably wouldn't apply solely to big decisions. Muller says that something as simple as a little girl sneaking out of her room and staring at her Christmas tree for fifteen minutes constitutes an event, in the physics sense. Once the light from the little multicolored bulbs on the tree and the photons reflecting off the wrapped gifts reach that girl's eyes, the event is done. Finished. Immutable. She has seen what she has seen, and her observation cannot be altered.

If time travel can't violate causality, which Muller suggests may be the case, this means that Santa's lieutenants can't travel back and visit that girl's living room during the time she was staring at the tree.

While he was busy with his other deliveries, she had already watched the tree and had not seen him. The event had already taken place.

Consider the following scenario involving one of Santa's favorite helpers, a jocular Norwegian named Knut. (Away from the North Pole, each of the lieutenants answers only to Santa, Kris, St. Nick, or other common nicknames, but Mrs. Claus and the OC refer to them by their given names. For purposes of clarity I'll do the same.) Let's say Knut is scheduled to visit this little girl's home at 12:02 A.M. Remember: Knut's 12:02 isn't her 12:02. Since Santa's lieutenants can travel back in time, Knut can let that first 12:02 elapse without worrying about falling behind. He can let time pass, and then return back to 12:02 to finish the job on time.

But if that little girl sits and stares at the tree from, say, midnight to 12:15, then her living room becomes off-limits. A time-travel no-fly zone. Knut couldn't go back in time to visit that room because the girl had already sat through those fifteen minutes without seeing him. An event, or observation, will have occurred, and Knut cannot overturn it. He wouldn't be able to visit that room because it would have already been established that he didn't. "This," according to Muller, "is why if little children get up and sneak a peek at the tree, Santa can't come."

Now, what if causality doesn't place these exact bounds on the lieutenants' rounds, and a few hundred children randomly step out into their living rooms and witness the same Santa, at the same "time"? What if each of these children simultaneously observes Knut? This implies that there are several hundred copies of the same person in different places in the world. Or it could mean that there are several hundred versions of our world existing in different universes at the same time, and in each one, Knut is in a different house, being witnessed by a different child.

Muller suggests that this possibility may have profound implications for the history of science. "The presence of Santa in many locations 'simultaneously' really bothered Einstein," he says. "I speculate that it was his wrestling with the Santa problem that really led Einstein to try to figure out the meaning of simultaneity. I am convinced that Santa's ability to travel in time led directly to Einstein's invention of relativity theory."

This is a provocative notion, and entirely plausible, but the important thing to consider here is what sort of bounds all of this places on Santa's rounds. Causality-related rules would add a whole new dimension of complexity to the travel schedule. If Knut's elfish coordinators fail to pick up on the fact that the little girl has ventured into the living room (unlikely, given all the in-home surveillance equipment that becomes operational on Christmas Eve) and do not provide him with a new route, what happens? Does the universe, anticipating a violation of causality, shut down the mouth of the wormhole that leads into the girl's living room? If this were the case, Knut might unknowingly dive into the other end of that wormhole, expecting to turn up in the girl's living room, and emerge in an alternate universe instead. He'd probably die. By sneaking a look at the tree, then, that little girl will have killed Santa. Or Knut, at least.

Yet it may be that the entire wormhole—both mouths and the tunnel that joins them—collapses. In this case, Knut would be forced to hit the pavement. His elfish minders would have to find him another wormhole, another way to resume his rounds, much like a bank robber who has to find a different escape route after the driver of his getaway car gets the jitters and bails. But how would causality apply here? Would Knut have to avoid being spotted by anyone? Could he not step on a single twig, kick a single stone or cigarette butt? And what's the difference between a girl witnessing him and some moonlight bouncing off his soft red hat—aren't they both events, in the physical sense? All valid questions, but unfortunately, these details are unavailable, and it would be intellectually and morally irresponsible to speculate.

But still. If these causality rules really do apply, then Knut would also have to worry about running into, or at least spotting, himself. Think about it. Say Knut finishes his rounds in house A, then slips through a wormhole into house B, which is right across the street. As he does so, he travels back in time roughly 29.99 seconds. So, when he emerges in house B, his former self will still be hard at work in house A. What if he decides to look through the window? What if he decides to just have a peek, to see whether the lights of that family's Christmas tree are favorable to his fair Norwegian complexion? It may be that the universe forbids the action. It may not even be possible. But Santa's elves take serious precautions to prevent his lieutenants from checking themselves out.

22

Time Travel and Delivery Tracking

HOW GPS PREVENTS SANTA FROM
RUNNING INTO HIMSELF

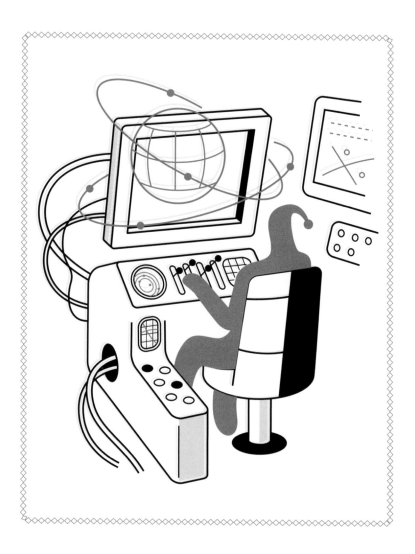

ELVES ARE QUITE possibly the most maligned, misunderstood group of Santa's helpers. Yes, they are hardworking, celibate, and short, but they are not simple craftsmen, as they are so often portrayed. Elves are highly skilled technical-support professionals, and in no area is this role more crucial than the scheduling of each Christmas Eve's deliveries. These tiny folk are masters of logistics.

Each Santa has to visit anywhere from 750,000 to one million homes, but, as we've established, the shortcuts created by wormhole-based time travel render the distance between two consecutive living rooms irrelevant. Since his lieutenants aren't really traveling through standard space-time, it's no faster for a given Santa to move from a mansion in Grosse Pointe, Michigan, to another across the street than it is for him to jump from there to a cabin in Belarus. As a result, each lieutenant's route actually covers a large stretch of the globe. Instead of going from house to house in a given neighborhood, he actually crisscrosses the planet to avoid running into any of his former selves.

The lieutenants don't accomplish this through some kind of heightened intuition. The elves plan out Santa's route in advance, and his travels are monitored and altered, if necessary, via the Lieutenant Santa Tracking System, or LiSTS, software program. To keep tabs on all those men, each Santa is outfitted with a highly precise GPS receiver. They don't work when the lieutenants are within a wormhole, but whenever a Santa is in our normal universe, inside a living room or studio apartment or mud hut, these high-powered devices repeatedly receive signals from a series of satellites, derive each lieutenant's precise coordinates, and feed them back to LiSTS to ensure each man is on schedule.

Now, the trick with this system is the fact that whenever a given Santa time-travels and reemerges in a new home, his receiver goes with him. From Knut's perspective, he only has one GPS device, and he keeps it with him the whole time as he moves from house to house.

But consider his elfish minder's point of view, sitting at his desk at the Pole. As Knut moves from the first house on his route to the second, he also skips back in time slightly less than thirty seconds. So, from the non-time-traveling elf's perspective, when he and his receiver arrive in the second house, he's still in the first one, too. And since Knut brings his receiver with him, the Pole's tracking system will register two copies of the same device. A second Santa will appear on the elf's screen. An instant later, after Knut time-travels again, rewinding another 29.9 seconds or so as he moves on to the third house, a third blip appears. From the perspective of LiSTS, there are now three exact copies of the same GPS receiver on the grid.

(Since GPS systems do depend on the accuracy of their clocks, the whole wormhole-time-travel technique did create a few technical headaches in the initial trials, but the elves, who have become incredibly skilled coders, fixed the bugs.)

The Pole's global map, which shows the locations of all copies of each Santa, is even more fantastic. If the whole operation starts with 267 Santas, then 267 GPS receivers leave the Pole to visit the first homes on their lists. Initially, 267 receivers register. Yet just a hundredth of a second or so later, after all those lieutenants have time-traveled for the first time, the number of receivers doubles and 534 devices turn up. A beat later, after the second clock-rewinding trip, that count doubles again, reaching 1,068.

What about causality? Good question. LiSTS was designed specifically to account for time-travel paradoxes; it positively gorges on memory as a result. But the elves are probably not allowed to follow these tracking dots on-screen. If they were to watch Knut for the first thirty seconds of his trip, for example, he wouldn't be able to rewind the clock as he moved to his next house. Because of these limitations, the elves do most of their work prior to Christmas Eve, when they plan each lieutenant's route in LiSTS. (Incidentally, Santa licenses a modified version of the software to UPS for package tracking. In fact, UPS executives regularly lead panel discussions on logistics at the Strategic Elvis Convention, which explains why they have, on more than one occasion, mistakenly slipped into Presley-esque accents at their own annual shareholder meetings and left investors amused but stupefied.) The program alerts them if any two points along a route are too close in space and time. When Santa and his lieutenants are actually out completing their rounds, LiSTS can adjust these routes autonomously. On rare occasions, though, the elves might be called upon to alert a given lieutenant that he has to change course or urge him to forgo an unscheduled nap (see the next chapter). But for the most part, they spend the evening watching Tim Allen's *Santa Clause* movies in their rooms. Why not sleep? They're too excited. In fact, none of Santa's workers get much rest on Christmas Eve.

23

Santa (Almost) Never Sleeps

WAKEFULNESS DRUGS, ANTI-SLEEP COMPOUNDS, AND EIGHT HOURS OF SHUT-EYE CRAMMED INTO A MINUTE

S ANTA AND HIS lieutenants rarely sleep during their Christmas Eve deliveries, but an hour or so is necessary here and there. They fight fatigue with a combination of brain-pod-released drugs that allow them to stay awake, working effectively, for several days at a clip. And that hour of shut-eye is an extremely powerful nap. It's the equivalent of eight to ten hours of normal sleep.

Clearly this alien-developed sleep-drug regimen is far beyond anything we have at our disposal today, but modern pill developers are making progress. Military studies have demonstrated that one of today's leading anti-sleep drugs, modafinil, allows people to remain alert and functioning for nearly forty-eight hours without any side effects. (Clubgoers have doubtless tested this even further, but the results of those studies have not been published.) The added bonus is that there's no need to catch up afterward, no need to lie in bed for a day to return to baseline. Patients can sleep for eight hours and wake up feeling fully restored.

Scientists aren't quite sure how modafinil and its upgrade, armodafinil, work their wonders, but the drugs appear to act on the brain's dopamine system. Unlike standard stimulants, though, they don't seem to lead to addiction. Another class of drugs, called ampakines, has also been shown to help maintain cognitive performance while keeping subjects awake. In one study, sleep-deprived monkeys that had been given an ampakine-based drug actually performed better on tests than subjects that had enjoyed a full night's rest.

These are just the pills that keep you awake, though. Scientists are also developing a new class of compounds that will guarantee a good night's sleep. Some of today's common sleep medications effectively just knock you out and make you think you had a good night's rest. They can leave you feeling drowsy and confused throughout the following day and prone to side effects like sleep-eating (which is kind of funny) and sleep-driving (not so funny). The effect is comparable to a college kid throwing back seven beers in the hour before he goes to bed. He might fall asleep instantly. He might not venture out of his room again for twelve hours. But that doesn't mean he's going to feel good when he does.

The goal of this new class of drugs, on the other hand, is to cram the very real physiological effects of a deep, long visit to dreamland into just a few hours. The recent advances in this field—both with sleep-promoting compounds and so-called wakefulness drugs like modafinil—have prompted some scientists to speculate that we could be headed toward a world in which sleep essentially becomes a choice. People will be able to remain awake for twenty-two hours, jam a full night's rest into the time it takes to watch a movie, and get up out of bed feeling perfectly restored.

Santa's molecular cocktail doesn't work quite in that way; the drugs released via the brain-pod delivery system that's surgically implanted in every new lieutenant keeps them alert and functioning fantastically for three days. After each seventy-one-hour period, during which a given lieutenant visits 8,520 homes, he stops and sleeps on one lucky family's living room couch for an hour. Then he's up and out and roaming through space-time again, completely refreshed and reenergized. Over the course of a given Christmas Eve, each Santa goes through roughly 95 cycles, working for a total of 6,745 hours while sleeping for just 95 hours. No wonder they don't mind hibernating when they're done.

The bug in this sleep/work program is free will. Each lieutenant retains it, and despite their nearly slavish dedication to the Christmas cause, on occasion, they decide to exercise it. Every once in a while, one of them realizes he really doesn't want to get back into the wormhole. He decides he wants to relax, lie down for a bit longer, maybe think about what Mrs. Claus will be wearing when she whips up her next batch of cookies. LiSTS repeatedly pings him with alerts (which he can see in the heads-up display in his spectacles), urging him to move on. If this fails, elves are brought in to reason with him. But he often tells them to go f!°$ a candy cane and wake him in another hour.

Time travel might seem like an easy solution to this problem. If one of these Santas takes an extra hour of rest, he can just travel back an extra hour to make it up, right? Yes, but he also increases the risk of running into one of his other selves. Remember: Every time Santa travels back in time, he essentially creates an extra version of himself. The initial lieutenant, who travels from the North Pole to the first house, creates a copy of himself when he travels back in time as he moves to the next house, because he's still in that first house, too.

Sure, LiSTS follows them all, but when one of these men decides to stay on the couch for a little longer than planned, he ruins all that logistical route-planning work his elfish handler completed beforehand. By changing the timing of everything, he risks encountering one of these time-travel-created copies of himself, who might be popping into a house across the street. In some instances, therefore, this apparently harmless refusal to rise from the couch forces LiSTS to rearrange massive numbers of deliveries. That can be incredibly stressful on the system; even alien software can crash.

You'd have to imagine that the lazy lieutenant would absolutely infuriate all the other copies of himself whose schedules he disrupts. At the same time, they'd probably get over it pretty quickly once they realized that it was really themselves that they were getting mad at. They might even sympathize and eventually conclude that they must have really needed the sleep.

So, although it is often said that the hardest person to forgive is yourself, when you're talking about a wormhole-time-travel-generated copy, this isn't really the case. It's actually pretty easy.

A Note About Whether or Not Reindeer Can Really Fly

No.

Reindeer and Public Relations

THE UNEXPECTED BENEFITS OF ENDANGERED SPECIES STATUS, AND WHY PUPPIES WOULDN'T BE MUCH GOOD AT PULLING SANTA'S SLEIGH

IF REINDEER CAN'T fly, why does Santa keep them around? Three reasons, one of which I can't divulge and another that we'll get to later. But first, and most important, he needs them for public relations.

The science and strategy of PR is complex enough when put to work for political figures, companies, and governments. But quasi-mythological figures require far more ingenuity. The closest analogue is celebrity PR, one of the goals of which is to convince, or at least remind, the fan base that the individual is, indeed, a real person, someone who plays with his or her kids, walks the dog, shops for groceries. The challenge with Santa is far grander, though, since he can't appear on talk shows or attend trendy parties or gallery openings or give glossy celebrity mags the chance to publish pictures of his goings-on about town. A central part of the Santa story is that he is not really a part of our world. He exists on the periphery, in secret, and visits only once per year. Granted, he can upgrade and sharpen his image through the publication of books or the production of Christmas-themed movies, but his only opportunity for direct, real-world PR presents itself on that single night. Therefore, his best opportunity to keep the story of Santa alive in the hearts and minds of children is to appear before them in all his jingling glory.

Cute and cuddly looking, reindeer are nearly ideal from a marketing perspective. The only creatures that score higher on emotional resonance tests are puppies, but Santa couldn't really have a puppy-drawn sleigh. Who would believe that? They're too small, too unfocused. Plus, it would be bad PR to have small animals pulling you around. It works them too hard.

At the same time, reindeer are also fairly impractical, which is why the OC is the only one of all the Santas who uses them. You don't need them to jump through a wormhole. They are loud, smelly, always hungry, and occasionally cantankerous. They're prone to defecating on rooftops, and it's the OC's responsibility to clean up their droppings, which, because they are spherical, and often frozen, have a tendency to roll down into the bushes that surround the average home. When this happens, Santa may end up wasting fifteen or twenty minutes scouring the shrubbery, digging through the snow in search of their crap. At least with puppies, the stuff would be small enough that he could just pretend it didn't happen. The homeowners would never notice.

Kids are another factor, of course. They just love reindeer. They love to hear the footsteps, the jingling of the bells on those leathery collars. They love to look across the way at a neighbor's house and see reindeer stomping over the slate roof, arching up and into the sky. They rush back into the house, alerting brothers, sisters, parents. The next morning they call their friends and cousins: "Santa is real! I saw him last night, with the sleigh and the reindeer and everything!"

Now, Santa wouldn't want just anyone making that call. To increase the impact of these eyewitness accounts, Santa generally tries to be seen mostly by influential children, those whom other kids would be more likely to believe. (His lieutenants, as we already established, try to avoid all contact, but since Santa doesn't time-travel, it's okay for him to be seen.) It wouldn't do much good, from a PR standpoint, to appear to a young fabulist, who might then be mocked at school for his testimony. Santa is also careful not to allow mentally or psychologically unstable children a glimpse, since he wouldn't want them screaming about the existence of Santa Claus only to have their parents whisk them to the doctor for an increased dose of medication. In this sense, Santa's operation functions less like a religion than a business. His public-relations effort is focused on leaders and decision-makers among the youth, not the downtrodden.

Yet children aren't his only target demographic. The OC also tries to ensure that a handful of environmentalists and animal biologists spot his reindeer each year, since the natural population of the beasts has been imperiled of late by climate change. Reindeer could become an endangered species if Earth's recent warming trend continues, and these appearances are Santa's way of informing environmentalists that he is on their side. He still has some work to do here, though, given his old ties to the coal industry.

But there's a gap in this story, an inconsistency, since we've already established that reindeer can't fly. If that's the case, how is it that these children and adults see them coasting off rooftops and into the night air? And how does the OC travel all the way from the North Pole if he's opposed to wormholes, anyway?

26

Turn Up the Warp Drive, Rudolph!

HOW SANTA USES EXTRADIMENSIONAL TRICKERY
TO SPEED ACROSS THE PLANET

A T ONE POINT in the movie *The Santa Clause*, the lead character, played by Tim Allen, stumbles when his son asks him how reindeer can fly. First he attributes this apparent capability to the aerodynamic effects of their antlers. Then he says that they're weightless. But Berkeley astrophysicist Richard Muller suggests that reindeer flight is actually an illusion. The reality, he says, is much simpler: "They're just really good leapers."

Now, he doesn't mean they can jump across states or countries. They don't get a big running start in Greenland and jump all the way to Green Bay. Instead, it may be that they can leap very well over short distances. From one rooftop to another that's close by, for example. It's not these short jumps that cause people to conclude that reindeer can fly, however. It's when the reindeer soar off the top of a house and seem to disappear. Witnesses assume that this apparent disappearance is an illusion. The reindeer must have accelerated to such a speed that they vanished. But that's not right at all. No, the roots of this flying-reindeer myth lie in Santa's warp-drive-powered sleigh.

Santa never stays in one neighborhood for very long, and on a given Christmas Eve, he likes to visit at least five continents and upwards of twenty countries. Even a rocket-powered sleigh wouldn't be fast enough to keep him on schedule. And, as we've mentioned already, he's opposed to wormhole-based time travel, so that's not an option, either. As a result, when Santa needs to get from one part of the world to another, he uses warp drive.

The big idea behind warp drive, a concept that turns up in countless science fiction novels and movies, from *Star Wars* to *Star Trek*, is fairly simple. Even though Albert Einstein imposed a kind of speed limit on the universe, insisting that nothing can move faster than the speed of light, or three hundred million meters per second, warp drive suggests that there might be a way around it. Instead of moving through space, you move space itself.

Think of one of those moving sidewalks in large airports and malls. There's probably a limit to how fast a human can run on the carpet alongside that people mover. But if you took the fastest man in the world, had him sprint for a stretch along that carpet, and then asked him to do the same on the moving sidewalk, he'd break his own record. In other words, he can only run so fast on the floor, but if you move the floor, too, he'll speed up.

Warp drive has a few different incarnations, but the models generally work according to this principle of moving space instead of moving through space. In one of the best-known models, the drive contracts the space-time in front of it and expands the space-time behind it. So, if you're trying to get from point A to B using this system, it effectively pushes A away from you and pulls B toward you. Rather than asking you to travel to your destination, it brings your destination to your doorstep.

Expanding, contracting, or warping space isn't simple, but it can be done. Planets, stars, and other massive bodies exert such a tremendous gravitational force on the space around them that they bend it, turning straight lines into curves. Doing this around a warp-drive ship, though, would require an equally enormous amount of energy packed into a much smaller space. In fact, one of the original warp-drive designs, proposed by Miguel Alcubierre in 1994, called for more energy than the universe has to offer. (Not to mention that this energy would actually have to be "negative energy," which might not even exist.) Still, it's not all bad news. Scientists have since revised Alcubierre's idea and brought those power requirements down to levels just short of impossible. They've also been thinking up clever new ways to actually make the warp drive work.

Recently, Baylor University physicists Richard Obousy and Gerald Cleaver proposed that it might be possible to expand and contract space by messing with the universe's extra dimensions. By "extra" they're referring to spatial dimensions other than the normal three we're accustomed to: width, depth, and height. Obousy and Cleaver say that expanding an extra dimension would lead to a contraction of space. Shrinking one, on the other hand, could end up causing that section of space to blow apart. So, the idea behind their warp drive is that if you could stretch one of these added dimensions in front of the ship—perhaps by using some variation of dark energy, the force that scientists think may be pushing the cosmos apart—and shrink one behind the ship, you'd push point A away from you and pull point B closer.

Yet this technique wouldn't be ideal for Santa. It would be too destructive. Obousy suggests thinking of the warp drive's route as a giant, elongated rectangle that stretches from your takeoff point to your destination. When the drive is switched on, the space between the ship and its destination is compacted. Everything in that rectangle is crushed.

Now imagine that Santa is making his rounds, and a passenger jet flies through his path. Since all that space would be shrunk to nearly nothing, the plane would be, too. Not a very merry Christmas for those passengers.

In reality, Santa's technology is closer to another recent warp-drive design, developed by the physicist Chris Van den Broeck. In this version, the drive encloses the ship in an isolated bubble of space-time, but this pocket universe is only connected to our normal, visible world by a tiny throat. If our world is that piece of paper we talked about in the wormhole chapter, the warp-drive bubble is a little balloon sitting on top, barely touching our universe.

As with wormholes, there aren't really any good analogies for this sort of phenomenon, since we're not really equipped to visualize extra dimensions or higher universes, but it might be worthwhile to consider the advantages of this model in terms of boats. Think of a standard jet as a tugboat. It sits low in the water and has to push a great deal of water out of the way to move, so it's slow. Van den Broeck's warp drive, in comparison, would be more like a hydrofoil, wherein only a fraction of the vehicle is actually touching the water. The hydrofoil and the warp-drive ship have less contact with the water and space-time, respectively, so it's easier for them to move.

There are safety advantages, too. Because the bubble's throat, or connection to our normal universe, is small, the warp drive's footprint in our world is tiny, too. As a result, the section of space it expands and contracts is also much smaller. That rectangle Obousy referred to shrinks in height and width. It's just a tremendously long sliver of space that gets crushed, and Santa avoids killing airline passengers and innocently coasting flocks of birds.

Warp drives aren't perfect. There are space limitations, for example. The larger the bubble, the more energy you need to create it. Santa's technology is highly advanced, but not even his tools can produce near-infinite amounts of negative energy.

Still, it works. When Santa's sleigh takes off, the warp drive generates a wormhole-like opening in the air. The reindeer pull Santa and his sleigh through, and they all slip into that isolated, balloonlike pocket of space-time. They slip out of the visible universe, travel almost instantly to the next destination, and pop back out again through another wormhole-like gate in the sky when it's time to land.

Muller suggests that this is the real source of the flying reindeer myth. Whenever a child sees the reindeer dropping down out of the night sky and landing on a rooftop, or soaring into the air with the sleigh trailing behind them, he or she is really watching as the animals, and the sleigh, slip into or out of a warp bubble. This creates the illusion that they're flying, but, as Muller notes, the truth is that they're just great leapers.

PART VI

Infiltration

27

Baby, It's Cold in Interdimensional Space

HOW SANTA'S SPACE SUIT KEEPS HIM ALIVE AND WELL IN EXTREME CONDITIONS

NOW THAT WE know how Santa spends his year, tracks kids, earns revenue, stays healthy, and gets around the world in practically no time, we can move on to more important matters. What does he wear?

Perhaps the most ridiculous of all the myths surrounding Santa Claus and his annual rounds is the idea that he accomplishes everything in a velour-like suit with thick leather boots, a belt, and a cuddly, fluff-trimmed hat. Wearing such an outfit would hardly be intelligent, given his mode of travel. No, Santa's suits are far more advanced than the stories and sketches suggest. But why do his lieutenants need to don the red if they avoid all contact with witnesses? Furthermore, why do baseball managers wear the same uniforms as players?

The second question is too great a mystery to address in such a short space, but Santa's lieutenants have a host of reasons for wearing the suits. First of all, they are optimized for space travel. Wormholes and warp drive both transport an individual out of Earth's atmosphere. They're still connected to our world, but it's likely that these regions of space-time do not have the same oxygen content and, as such, aren't great places for humans, even ones with powerful health plans, to spend much time. Remember, the OC travels in an open-air sleigh. And his lieutenants don't even use a vehicle: They just jump from one living room to the next, in and out of all those wormhole mouths. These journeys are often very brief, on the order of a few seconds or less, so a given Santa holds his breath as he slips into and out of an alternate world.

The suits also offer protection should something go wrong. Say, for example, the tunnel is slightly longer than expected, or the warp drive isn't purring perfectly. Santa's suits, which, from the outside, do appear to resemble the fluffy, blanketlike versions depicted in so many illustrations and movies, can be sealed and offer a forty-five-minute supply of oxygen. By pulling his hat down over his face and attaching the stretchable brim to his collar, Santa can activate a pressurization system and allow himself some time to breathe.

This is primarily for emergencies. Wormhole malfunctions lead to approximately one Santa every two years finding himself lost in an alternate universe. As far as we know, this never really ends well. But on the rare occasion that one of these unlucky Santas pops out of a busted wormhole somewhere in our galaxy, the suit gives him a chance for survival. Since the suit is pressurized and provides air for him to breathe, he knows he can live for a time, so he depresses an emergency response button. (It's the third one from the top.) The suit then sends signals in all directions, which Santa's space-based observatories eventually pick up. These observatories triangulate the signal and forward the estimated location of the lost Santa to the North Pole. Once the relevant elves are alerted, they inform the OC. If the lieutenant in question is close enough, the OC cranks up the warp drive and picks him up.

Now, I know what you're thinking: Why does he have to be close? If the OC has warp drive, couldn't he go anywhere in the universe in a matter of minutes? Possibly, yes. But the OC is more concerned with time than distance. The OC could get to this Santa in a flash, but there's no point if his oxygen has already run out. The problem is that the stranded Santa's distress signal travels at the speed of light. Down here on Earth, three hundred million meters per second is quick enough for emergency communications. But space presents a different scale. It takes eight minutes for light from the Sun to reach Earth, and the Sun is practically next door—just about ninety-three million miles away. Since the stranded Santa has forty-five minutes' worth of oxygen in his tank, that distress signal has a little bit more time to travel, but he's still going to have to be somewhere within the Milky Way galaxy. If he pops out of that wormhole a few billion miles from Earth, there's no hope. His oxygen reserves will be gone by the time the North Pole's observatories receive the signal, and he'll be long dead when the OC pulls up in his warp-drive sleigh.

(Time travel probably wouldn't work here either, since the universe doesn't allow Santa to change events that have already happened. Unless, of course, nobody observes the death, in which case there might be some tree-falling-in-the-forest, causality-related way of getting around that apparent rule. But that's for the aliens to figure out.)

The suits also have a number of other capabilities. They are flame-proof, which, given the fact that Santa is constantly jumping into fireplaces, is pretty important. A stain- and moisture-resistant layer of fabric sits on the outside, so spilled eggnog trickles right off the suit and down to the floor. The furry white brim can be pulled down and attached to the collar, as described above, but it also contains an earpiece and microphone so that a given Santa may consult directly with one of his elfish minders if necessary.

This is only allowed in emergencies, though; most of the time, communication flows strictly in one direction, with the AI software that coordinates all of Santa's activities issuing orders through e-mail directives and other alerts.

Those quaint little reading glasses so often depicted on the end of Santa's nose? Look closely and you'll see that the lenses are embedded with circuitry. The glasses function as a heads-up display, so that when Santa peers through them, he sees a virtual projection of his tasks, agenda, next steps, or any urgent warnings.

The suits also boast a collection of wonderful little hidden pockets. Generally, Santa's lieutenants find them stylish, breathable, and flattering. Yet the OC doesn't endow his lieutenants' suits with all the best technology. In fact, he keeps the finest materials for himself.

28

The Instantly Invisible Man

METAMATERIALS, HOME INFILTRATION, AND
THE SHOTGUN-SWINGING DAD PROBLEM

Though it's important for Santa to let himself be seen on occasion, there are moments when he would prefer to disappear. In the home of an overprotective father, for example. Take the following hypothetical.

Still lying awake after spending the last few hours setting presents under the tree, Dad hears a noise in the living room. He swings his legs out of bed. He just saw a program on the news about Christmas burglars, and he isn't going to let them grab his family's goodies.

His wife wakes and whispers to him. He lifts a single finger to his lips, telling her to be quiet. Up off the bed, Dad reaches inside his old terry-cloth bathrobe and removes the loaded shotgun he keeps there for these sorts of potential emergencies and/or invasions by foreign powers, be they Russian or North Korean. He tiptoes down the stairs, hears more rustling below.

The OC, at this point, is still scanning the scene, making sure he has everything in order. But then he hears a click. Carefully, slowly, and, as always, jovially, he turns and sees a flannel-pajama-dressed Dad pointing a loaded shotgun in his direction.

In an instant he disappears from view. He's still in the room, in the same spot as before, in fact. But he has become invisible, thanks to the metamaterials in his suit. His futuristic threads bend light around him instead of reflecting or absorbing it. They're not the only things in the universe that have this ability. Stars, for example, exert so much gravitational force on the space-time around them that they actually warp it. A straight line extending past a star isn't really straight, from our standpoint, but curved. Light loops right around them. Santa's metamaterials have the same effect, but on a local level. They reroute light and hide him from view.

In recent years, researchers have begun edging closer to developing materials with the phenomenal capabilities of Santa's suit. Duke University scientist David Smith and John B. Pendry of Imperial College London, two of the pioneers in the field, laid the theoretical foundation for a real-world cloaking device in 2006. This mathematical work was a critical first step, but the scientists didn't wait long to move into the construction phase. Less than a year later, Smith and his group at Duke constructed a device that reroutes microwave radiation around a hockey-puck-sized object. More recently, Ames National Laboratory physicist Costas Soukoulis and his colleagues at Karlsruhe University reported that they had developed a material that has the same effect on visible light.

Despite the accelerated progress in these last few years, a few significant challenges remain. None of these early incarnations would work with moving objects. They couldn't make someone the size of Santa disappear. They generate distortions that someone with decent vision would have no trouble discerning. Plus, the designs are generally optimized for specific frequencies. This is a problem because visible light—the stuff that our eyes pick up—includes a wide range of wavelengths. Blocking out just one frequency wouldn't be enough. Santa wouldn't feel very safe if only the red portions of his suit became invisible and not the black belt and white trim. Currently, though, there is no design that can manipulate more than one kind of light.

Yet Santa's suit works across the spectrum. When Dad initially steps into the living room, he sees Santa because the light in the room is reflecting off the suit, and the OC, and traveling toward his eyes. Dad's brain then makes sense of this colorful picture and tells him there's a guy kneeling before his tree, sorting through his kids' presents.

Now, how does Santa disappear? Normally, one of three things happens to light when it strikes an object. The light is either reflected, absorbed, in which case it turns into heat, or transmitted, meaning that it passes straight through. Windows mostly transmit light; mirrors reflect it. But metamaterials actually bend the light.

Imagine that Santa is crouched directly between Dad and the tree. Before he disappears, light from different sources—a lamp on the table, the tree lights, the moon—strikes his suit and reflects in different directions, including right at Dad's eyes. When the metamaterials in Santa's suit are activated, however, this light actually flows around the OC, like the water in a river flowing around a boulder.

If Dad were to take two flashlights, hold them side by side, and shine them right at Santa's midsection, the suit would channel the two beams around him, one to the left and the other to the right, then allow them to reemerge and resume their course, and their parallel alignment, on the other side of him. The light would effectively ignore Santa Claus.

Eventually the beams would bounce off the needles and ornaments of the tree behind him. Some of the light would head back the way it came and loop around Santa, once more acting as if he wasn't there, before finally reaching Dad's eyes. At this point, Dad's brain would process the visual data and inform him that there was only a tree before him and not an intruder. In effect, the metamaterials make the scene behind Santa (the section of the tree he's blocking) visible, so that it looks like he's not there.

Standing now in what would seem to be an entirely empty room, this very defensive father uncocks his shotgun and rubs his eyes. This proves ineffective, as metamaterials are even impervious to eye rubbing. He questions his sobriety and his sanity. He thinks back to earlier that night. How many glasses of eggnog did he have? Hmmmm. And then there was the champagne later in the night as they were sorting the presents, after the kids had gone to sleep.

Confused, Dad returns to bed. Santa, still cloaked, hurries away and makes a note not to return. Yet he survives. He avoids a shotgun blast and preserves his life.

Such encounters are rare. More often than not, Santa is aware of sleepwalking parents and kids long before they make it into the living room, thanks in large part to the all-seeing eye at the top of each tree.

29

Quiet, the Ornaments Are Listening

SCANNING FOR INTRUDERS AND WITNESSES
VIA AUDIO AND VIDEO SURVEILLANCE

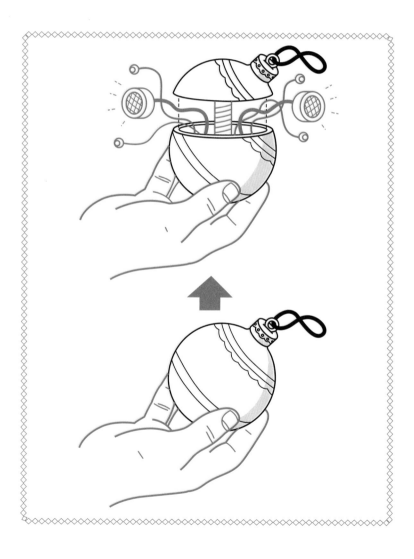

T HE STAR ATOP the average Christmas tree appears to be just another ornament, but it's actually a highly advanced surveillance device designed to ensure that Santa minimizes unanticipated run-ins during his deliveries. These devices are also crucial for the time-traveling lieutenants. They pick up on children sneaking out to peek under the tree and alert the elves, who can block out that time period and ensure that no lieutenants attempt to visit that home and risk bumping into the aforementioned causality issue.

Santa has ties to an astonishing number of companies, but thanks to Mrs. Claus, he's always been particularly involved in the ornament industry. (The popular designer Christopher Radko and he are very good friends, for example.) This is partially a Christmas-spirit issue; he wants to ensure that ornaments convey holiday cheer and charity. But, as described in previous chapters, many of these decorative elements also contain highly sensitive listening devices. Still, for Christmas Eve, Santa relies on much more versatile technology.

Typically, the equipment is embedded in treetop ornaments, since these offer the best vantage point. Each one of these has two main sensors. One is optical, the other auditory. Take the standard treetop angel. The figure's eyes double as miniature stereo cameras. With each lens acting as a different "eye" and recording an event from a different perspective, they can capture both 3-D video and still images. When the technology is built into a decorative star, each camera lens, or eye, is situated on an opposing point and concealed by a decorative element, such as an imitation gemstone. The function, though, remains the same.

Typically the video data is processed inside the ornament, in a miniature computer. Certain events—a little girl checking out what's been left under the tree, for example—are red-flagged, and the relevant image or video clip is then routed back to the North Pole for analysis. These devices have proven effective, but Santa has also begun releasing models that take advantage of home Wi-Fi systems. Rather than process all the information internally, the angel sends the raw data back to the North Pole via the homeowner's Wi-Fi connection. The advantage here is threefold. Santa can package the surveillance equipment in smaller ornaments, since there's no need for a robust processor. The devices also burn less energy, given that they don't have to crunch all that data on-site, so they extend their battery life. Finally, they don't need very powerful antennae, since they're only sending data across a room and not halfway around the world. (There are rumors up at the Pole about the possibility of Santa leaving fewer presents at homes without Wi-Fi networks because of the headaches these tech-averse destinations create.)

This video information, which Santa also uses for performance-review purposes, running through little missteps or oversights on the part of his lieutenants (which the elves are only too happy to point out), is crucial. It can provide clear-cut evidence that a child or adult is present in Santa's target landing area, the living room. But on its own it would not suffice.

The OC needs to know when people are in the room, yes, but he also needs to know when they are on their way. If he's about to land his warp-drive ship on someone's roof, rappel down the wall, and climb in through a window (the whole squeezing-through-the-chimney bit is a myth; honestly, does anyone think that's really even remotely possible?), he wants to be warned if a little girl is tiptoeing down the hall at the same moment, or if an overaggressive father is awake and on guard.

To pick up these often gentle footfalls, the ornaments use a sensor system very similar to one that's currently being tested as a military sniper detector. The RedOwl system features laser range finders, thermal imagers, and more, but the key element is a listening device developed by Boston University scientist Socrates Deligeorges. It consists of a microphone array and a processor that can almost instantly determine the source and nature of a given sound. A series of four microphones sit at the four corners of the boxlike device. If someone fires a gun within its hearing range, the pressure waves generated by the event register in each of the four microphones. An onboard computer then translates this data and estimates, based on the time each microphone received the signal, where the sound originated. The first incarnations of the RedOwl's sniper finder fit inside a hardcover-book-sized package, but the researchers estimate that they'll be able to scale that down to something the size of two cigarette packs.

Santa's version is smaller still, and highly sensitive. Whereas the angel's "eyes" can only pick up people inside the room, its "ears" can hear them approaching. Deligeorges and his colleagues trained Red-Owl to distinguish between different sounds; it can correctly identify not just where a gun was fired, but what kind of gun was fired. Similarly, Santa's in-house ears can estimate whether footsteps belong to a parent or child, and if they're the hesitant, creeping brand taken by someone on an illicit mission or the heavy, sleepy kind that occur when someone is simply headed to the bathroom in the middle of the night.

All of this technological backup isn't always necessary; most of Santa's drop-offs proceed smoothly. (That's why they call it backup.) And that's really the point of his extensive surveillance network. It allows Santa to focus on his real work: delivering gifts.

PART VII

Delivery

30

How Santa Knows What You Want

A FTER SANTA SLIPS into a room, he settles down in front of the tree and determines which present or presents to deposit beneath the glowing, multicolored lights. This isn't a guess or a decision made on a whim. But it's not precalculated, either.

As we've detailed, he has tremendous surveillance capabilities. In the absence of an official, written list sent via mail to the North Pole, Santa could certainly tap into phone calls, e-mails, even certain school-yard conversations to figure out which toys a child wants. Yet this information wouldn't really do Santa much good. The important thing here is not simply what the kid wants, but which presents their parents neglect or fail to provide for them. As any sane adult understands, Santa does not give us all of our Christmas gifts. He only leaves those which our parents could not afford or simply forgot to provide. So, if Mom and Dad give us nine of the ten presents, Santa has to be sure that he drops off that missing tenth gift. He can't just pick anything off the list because he'll risk doubling up and leaving a little kid two of the same American Girl doll, for example.

One way to avoid such a potentially devastating Christmas-morning scenario—one that could provoke an argument between husband and wife over who was so ignorant as to purchase that extra doll, an argument that could very well bring other marital issues to the fore and spark a massive fight, ruining Christmas and possibly the next few decades of life for the innocent kids—would be to monitor credit-card transactions and implement a software program that can cross-reference the itemized receipts with the child's wish list. That way, Santa would be able to see which gifts Mom or Dad purchased and which ones were left off. The problem here is that parents are forgetful. Presents are sometimes purchased months in advance, stashed deep in the attic or some hidden nook in the garage, and then completely forgotten about. A longed-for GI Joe might be left in a box, which can lead to the intended recipient feeling broken with disappointment on Christmas morning, not that this author has any experience with such things. The point here is that the purchase of a gift does not necessarily guarantee that it will end up under the tree. This system simply isn't viable.

Santa needs a more direct way of assessing a given child's haul. He needs to rapidly and accurately determine what is inside each wrapped box and figure out which additional presents to leave based on that information. Basically, he needs a T-ray scanner.

T-rays, or terahertz radiation waves, sit between microwave and infrared on the electromagnetic spectrum. Microwaves are longer, infrared shorter. Both of these are fairly common in our everyday lives. We use microwaves to reheat leftovers, and infrared radiation, among other things, allows us to stay seated as we flip through cable channels. So, if these two are so popular, why isn't anyone using the band of light that sits between them? Is terahertz radiation the electromagnetic spectrum's version of the middle child, forgotten and ignored? Perhaps, but the psychology of radiation research is not our concern here. The primary reason that terahertz radiation has been so underutilized is that it's difficult to generate.

Today's most promising terahertz source, according to senior scientist Jason Dickinson of the University of Massachusetts–Lowell, is the quantum-cascade laser, or QCL. Dickinson says the QCL is the equivalent of a laser pointer for T-rays. But for it to work, it needs to be cooled down to just four degrees above absolute zero. This makes the technology quite a bit more complicated than a handheld laser pointer.

But there's still a tremendous interest in the field. "Companies and governments are looking for better ways to perform discreet security-type inspections, especially at airports," Dickinson says. Terahertz waves are ideal because they lack the energy of X-rays and are thus far less harmful to cells. You can repeatedly blast someone with T-rays, and you won't have to worry about kick-starting cancer. They can also pass through a range of materials, including plastics, clothing, and more. The two things that do stop them are water and metal, which is a benefit when you're looking for hidden weapons. If someone harboring a gun were to walk through a T-ray scanner at the airport, the radiation would shine right through his clothes, then bounce back once it ran into the metal gun or the water-filled tissues in his body. A terahertz-based device could also detect a range of other substances, including bomb-making materials, by detecting the unique radiation signals of the components.

Santa's device is portable, battery operated, and delightfully user-friendly. He carries it in the sack thrown over his shoulder and removes it once he settles into a given living room. Time is critical for Santa, so the device has to work fast. Modern T-ray technology would not suffice; you might be able to use it to compile a full-body scan of a person, for example, but it would probably take at least a few minutes. Even if Santa had to focus his scanner on a single item for two seconds, that means it would take him a full minute or more to register all the presents in the home of a medium-sized, upper-middle-class family.

His T-ray system works much faster; typically he scans the room once, in about three seconds, and then waves the device back over the same area for another two seconds. The device both pumps out and receives the radiation. The different materials in the wrapped gifts—papers, plastics, cardboard, etc.—either transmit the T-rays, allowing them to pass straight through; absorb them; or kick them back toward the device. Santa's scanner receives that reflected radiation, then wirelessly transmits the raw data back to the North Pole's server farm.

Next, Santa's computers run that information through a toy ID program. Given the radiation data, the program computes the precise size and shape of a given toy. It also breaks down its molecular composition, since the materials inside all have specific spectral signatures. The toy ID program compares all of this information with the prerecorded shapes and material compositions of all known toys and dolls and gifts. It effectively runs a search, looking for popular toys with the same physical characteristics, and computes a match.

Dickinson guesses that the system probably isn't perfect, since a terahertz-based gift identifier would have difficulty distinguishing a toy packed inside a cardboard box. It would be far more successful with trucks or dolls that have plastic covers and cardboard backing. Yet given Santa's sterling reputation for knowing what kids want, it must be that his toy ID program and scanning device make use of some technological shortcuts around these obstacles.

Once the system identifies each of the gifts scanned, it cross-references this information with the child's wish list to see which items are missing and, finally, routes the data back to Santa. Seconds after he scans the presents, the heads-up display in his reading glasses returns a report. Looking through his spectacles, he sees which toy or toys he's supposed to leave. And this is where Santa's tech gets truly interesting.

What Really Happened at Tunguska

WHY A SUPPOSED METEORITE EXPLOSION IS
REALLY SANTA'S FAULT

O N JUNE 30, 1908, a massive explosion occurred in a remote forest in Siberia. An estimated eighty million trees were knocked down, covering an area of more than eight hundred square miles. No direct eyewitness accounts of the explosion were recorded, but plenty of people testified to its effects. There were changes in the sky as far away as England, and several hundred miles from the blast site, locals reported being thrown to the ground by the shock wave. The air became incredibly bright and hot. Trees caught fire. Buildings shook, and several people compared the sounds they heard to artillery fire.

Scientists and conspiracy theorists have been debating what happened at that remote spot in Siberia, called Tunguska, ever since. The theories range from the explosion of a meteorite fragment a few miles above the ground (plausible) to a collision of a large chunk of invisible, exotic dark matter with the Earth's surface (not so plausible). No one has considered that Santa might have been involved.

The aliens provided Santa with a set of very easy-to-read operations manuals that spell out how to use each of his many technologically advanced toys. They also told him to read them only in case of emergency, since they designed everything to be very simple to operate, knowing that the OC was technologically clueless. But at one point he got a little too confident. Like any prolific gadget user, he decided to ignore the manual and determine how to work a device, and what to use it for, on his own. This yielded disastrous results.

The tool he chose to test was called a replicator. It released thousands of micromachines that acted in concert, according to a central directive. Santa thought it might be an alternative means of

manufacturing toys, particularly wooden trains. (They were still popular in 1908.) The device had a simple user interface: All he had to do
was hold up the item he wished to have copied and rotate it in front of
a built-in scanner. Next, he figured he'd just press the green button
tagged "GO" and watch the gadget work. The technology, he decided,
would be perfect: easy to use and portable, too. He was thinking he
could keep it in the sleigh and create toys out of the firewood stacked
in so many family backyards. Then he could just leave the toys where
they were. His intentions were noble; he thought it would be fun for
kids if gifts turned up in unexpected places.

Santa's assessment of his own technological abilities was severely
misguided at the time, so when Mrs. Claus learned of his plan, she
insisted that he first test it at a remote location. This in itself wasn't
unreasonable. Travel was no issue for Santa. His warp-drive sleigh
could carry him to Antarctica in the same time it would take him to
walk across his bedroom to the toilet.

He chose that remote spot in Siberia, set the device on the dirt in
the middle of a thick grove of trees, and pressed GO. The replicator
immediately released a swarm of thousands of micromachines, each
just a fraction of the size of a potato bug. They surrounded the nearest
tree, and its base quickly became a cloud of sawdust. Seconds later, as
the thin wood chips settled, an exact replica of the toy caboose Santa
wanted to copy lay on the floor. He was ecstatic. He was so proud of
himself, in fact, that he decided to sit back and enjoy a pipe, an activity
that Mrs. Claus had already barred at the North Pole.

Soon, though, he realized something wasn't quite right. The micromachines weren't stopping. They moved in a circular pattern from
tree to tree, transforming a chunk of wood at the base of each one into
a toy caboose and causing the trees to topple. Before Santa could even
think to act, the machines had felled thousands of trees. And they only
seemed to be moving faster. Soon it was as if a massive explosion had
taken place. In a panic, he dropped his pipe, and the discarded bits of
branch and wood all around him caught fire. His warp-drive sleigh
exploded, producing that tremendous shock wave.

Eventually he grabbed a large stone and began smashing the
micromachines, one by one, until there wasn't a single one left. By the

time he was finished, more than eight hundred square miles of the forest had been swallowed and burned, and Santa was forced to walk around picking up the freshly carved wooden cabooses that hadn't been incinerated.

The device was now useless, given that he had flattened all the micromanufacturers. Worse yet, when he lifted it, along with all the new toys, into his sack for the long walk him home, he saw a red button on the back that read "STOP."

Santa, naturally, has not come forward as the true culprit behind the Tunguska event. In fact, he has moved beyond this incident and all but erased it from his memory. Indeed, he has replaced many of his organs since then; in a ship-of-Theseus sort of way, the current Santa isn't even really responsible. The whole thing was a mistake. The truth is that he didn't need the device in the first place. He didn't need to worry about making gifts, whether they were trains, dolls, or complex, many-colored Transformers.

His toys manufacture themselves.

32

Toys That Build Themselves

ON-DEMAND MANUFACTURING VIA
DIRECTED SELF-ASSEMBLY

SANTA COULDN'T LUG around finished toys. That just wouldn't make sense. Even the largest bag would only be able to hold twenty to twenty-five items. And because of the fact that he never knows which toys he's going to leave until he aims that scanner at the presents under the tree and determines which gifts the child has already received from their parents, he would need to haul nearly all of his options into every house. If little Cindy Cornue on Beach Road in Tequesta, Florida, has seven toys on her wish list, Santa would have to bring all seven. Now imagine that Santa determines he should leave toy number 3. That's fine, but if he then heads to the next house and learns that Shawnie Cox should also be given toy number 3, he would either have to head back to the North Pole, bust into a local toy store, grab the item, and leave an IOU (a serious violation of his public relations credo), or carry doubles of everything. Regardless, this method wouldn't be very smart. In some cases he might only cover two or three homes before needing to restock.

We also know that the elves do not actually make the toys, and that Santa doesn't buy them wholesale, or even at a discounted rate. Either way, this would be far too expensive. Even if the major toy manufacturers were kind enough to sell Santa the toys at 20 percent of the suggested retail price, the total could run to several billion dollars. That's not even taking into account the transportation costs, whether he were to have the items shipped to the North Pole or dispersed among regional distribution centers across the world. Santa has money, but not that much.

For the most part—possible exceptions will be addressed in the next chapter—the toys and dolls and other items Santa leaves assemble themselves. (And no, they're not robots or anything like that. They're not going to suddenly morph from Barbie dolls into killer machines that threaten to take over your house if you don't give them remote control rights. Which, by the way, you should never do, because, being humanoids, they will probably only want to watch reruns of the 1980s sitcom *Small Wonder.*) Self-assembly is actually very common, and Santa's isn't the only operation that finds it useful.

Some experts think it will be the manufacturing technique of the future, and several accomplished researchers are making major strides with it today. The renowned Harvard chemist George Whitesides has highlighted the potential of self-assembly by pointing to nature. From the life-sustaining machines in the cell to massive galaxies, nature is filled with living and inorganic structures that build themselves. Nobody watches over these growth or formation processes, ushering them along. A program kicks into gear, whether it's written in DNA or astrophysical constants, and cells, galaxies, trees, plants, and animals emerge.

Chemists, biologists, and materials scientists have been working with self-assembling molecules for years, but now researchers are also trying to use the approach to build larger, more complex structures. One of the driving forces behind the research is the fact that the components that lie at the heart of those wonderful gadgets we so often take for granted are constantly shrinking. Babak Parviz, an electrical engineer at the University of Washington, says that a typical microprocessor has more than five hundred million parts crammed into a space of less than one square inch. These parts are roughly a thousand times thinner than a strand of hair.

And that's just the situation today. These pieces will continue to shrink, and they'll also become more complex. Future microprocessors could include not just electrical components, but biological and chemical pieces, too. As a result, they will become increasingly difficult to manufacture. Today's conventional manufacturing techniques, Parviz says, will not be able to handle this level of complexity.

Yet nature does far more difficult work all the time, governing the construction of systems with trillions of components. Therefore, Parviz and others are trying to emulate nature. They want to grow machines.

Among other things, Parviz and his group have already produced high-performance circuits made of semiconductors—the fundamental building blocks of modern electronics—through self-assembly. Okay, so this isn't quite a PC or an iPhone, but it's a step forward, and the work is starting to teach them what it will take to get more complex man-made components or devices to slap themselves together. First, you need to pick out the building blocks, the pieces that are actually going to join to form the finished product. Then you need to figure out how to link them up in the right way and in the correct places. Finally, you have to decide how the whole process is going to be governed. What physical forces or laws will help you progress toward that finished product?

In one experiment, Parviz and his group wanted to embed a number of LEDs, or light-emitting diodes, in a plastic contact lens. They added very tiny wires to a plastic lens and also included, at different points along those wires, round depressions in the surface that matched the size and shape of the circular LEDs. After some prep work, the lens was placed in solution, and a group of LEDs was left to repeatedly drift through the fluid over the surface. The LEDs fell into the circular depressions, and the lens was removed when each hole was filled. (In other words, they waited until the round lights fell into the round holes.) Next they heated the lens, and the LEDs bonded to the surface. The result was an LED-equipped contact lens that had partially assembled itself.

Not to insult Parviz and his contemporaries, but Santa's equipment is far more advanced and hews much closer to the efficiency of mother nature's technique. The major upgrade, and a necessary one at that, is speed. Trees do build themselves, but it takes them a long time. Santa wouldn't be able to wait months or years for a present to put itself together; he needs his toys to assemble in a few hours or less.

Let's get back to little Cindy in Tequesta. When Santa turns up at her house and uses the scanner to determine which gift he should leave under the tree, he doesn't have to search through his bag for the correct item. He pulls out a single wrapped and bow-tied box.

(He used to have two options, one with girl-themed wrapping and another with the paper geared toward boys, but Mrs. Claus insisted that this sent the wrong sort of message about her husband's social awareness, informing him that he might as well just leave the boys guns and the girls aprons. He eventually adopted gender-neutral, Christmas-tree-filled, green-and-red paper instead.)

Inside, a self-assembly apparatus awaits a signal. Santa types the given gift's product code (which he gets from the toy ID program) into his remote control. He aims it at the box, and the process begins. The relevant building blocks are released into a central, solution-filled chamber, and, over the course of the next few hours, they gradually link together to form more complex higher-order structures. The toy assembles first, and the leftover components, or building blocks, merge to form the proper container, whether it be plastic, metal, or cardboard. Finally, the solution drains out through a virtually undetectable hole in the bottom of the box and evaporates quickly, leaving little or no trace on the carpet or hardwood floors.

(Some of the newer-model composite hardwoods from IKEA tend to react with the solution, resulting in a slight fade in the color of the faux wood, but Santa's elves are working to remedy this unfortunate consequence. On a different but equally tangential note, you might have noticed that one of the flaws with self-assembly is that each apparatus is a one-time-use device. That is, Santa, or his lieutenants, have one less self-assembly device every time they visit a house. And this, in turn, might have incited you to wonder what happens when Santa runs out, given that his bag doesn't contain an infinite volume of space. The answer, sadly, is fairly boring. Additional self-assembly devices are stored in warehouses across the world; Santa and his lieutenants have to visit them frequently, via wormhole or warp drive, to restock, which only makes travel coordination that much more difficult.)

Without these self-assembling toys, it's conceivable that Santa would not be able to complete his annual rounds at all. Yet the technology is not perfect. It could not produce every gift Santa drops off on a given Christmas Eve. In certain cases, the toys are too complex, and Santa needs to turn to a more powerful manufacturing device.

Every once in a while, Santa needs a PERM.

33

Teleporting Kittens

PORTABLE ENTANGLEMENT-BASED RAPID MANUFACTURERS
AND OTHER TELEPORTATION-DERIVED APPLICATIONS

SANTA ONLY USES his PERM, or Portable Entanglement-based Rapid Manufacturer, when faced with impossible-to-manufacture gifts. Some items are too difficult to build piece by piece or to search out at the last minute. Like kittens. Santa loves dropping off kittens; the kids adore them, and the parents can't say no to them. But his self-assembly tech can't handle living organisms, and Mrs. Claus is allergic to cats, so he can't keep a stock of them at the Pole.

Instead of creating each of these specialty items, or buying up and stockpiling them during the year, Santa teleclones them. Using his PERMs, he simultaneously creates thousands of copies of a single item in living rooms across the world.

Telecloning is based on the phenomenon of entanglement, a long-postulated and recently confirmed trick that nature plays in the quantum world. The study of entanglement started out as an imaginative argument between two of the greatest scientists of the twentieth century, Albert Einstein and Niels Bohr, only one of whom believed in Santa Claus. Ultimately, it says that if two little bits of matter or photons of light are linked in a certain way, messing with one of them will instantly affect the other as well. The actual how-it-works details are considerably more complex, in part because physicists like to use terms that have one meaning in our world but a different one in theirs. For example, although subatomic particles are neither tasty nor dreidel-like, physicists say they have qualities like "flavor" and "spin." When two particles are entangled, adjusting the spin of one changes the spin of the other. But, again, it's not that kind of spin.

Instead of discussing spinning electrons that don't really spin, we'll put this in more Santa-friendly terms. Say Mrs. Claus has two small chocolate-chip cookies. Being a woman of moderation, she decides that they are still too much for her alone, so she places each one in the center of its own plate. She sets one plate on the kitchen table, then carries the other over to her husband's desk.

When Mrs. Claus returns to her kitchen, she sits down and, noticing that her cookie is situated slightly off center, she moves it to the right. (She has a mild case of OCD; the upside of this is that her hair is always perfect.) If these two cookies are entangled, then Santa's will move at exactly the same time.

This is the general idea, anyway; the real truth is that scientists haven't actually figured out if entanglement would work at the cookie level. For now, this phenomenon, which Einstein called "spooky action at a distance," is limited to the microworld. Physicist Anton Zeilinger of the University of Vienna was one of the first to prove that entanglement is real, but in the last decade, many more scientists have jumped into the strange new field. They've entangled photons of light and even clouds of particles, and, by acting on one part of the pair, induced instant changes in the other. *Star Trek*–style teleportation isn't quite on the horizon, but these scientists—at the University of Maryland, MIT, Georgia Tech, and other leading institutions—contend that their work with quantum entanglement could soon lead to unbreakable codes and faster computers.

In a slightly different twist, a group at the University of York, led by physicist Sam Braunstein, entangled three groups of particles in such a way that measuring one induced a change in the other two. This was the first case of quantum telecloning, the process by which two, three, and even four copies of an original are produced via entanglement. The exciting point: Braunstein and his team suggest in their paper that there is no limit to the number of possible clones. And this is where we get back to Santa.

Each PERM contains a cloud of entangled particles inside a gift-wrapped shell. Each device and each collection of particles it contains is linked to those inside an original, or master, PERM at the North Pole. When Santa finds that a child desires a gift that can't be self-assembled, he deposits a PERM. (If he runs out, he picks up new ones at the nearest warehouse.) At the end of the night, when his rounds are complete, one of the elves back at the Pole entangles the desired item with that master PERM. The essential information is transferred to that device and then dispatched to each of the entangled PERMs across the world. In a flash, hundreds, or even thousands, of those items, whether they be kittens or vintage robots, materialize.

Seriously? Is this really how it works? Does Santa really teleclone toys and pets? No. Santa does take advantage of quantum entanglement, but only with his computers; it's one of the reasons his AI programs are so robust and his servers can churn through and analyze so much data. Sadly, PERM-style teleportation of the sort described here, though incredibly appealing, is probably not possible in our universe.

But everything else in this book is true.

Acknowledgments

Nika, for love, support, confidence. Clare and Eleanor, for horse-play and other welcome diversions. Mom and Dad, for the Millennium Falcon and so much more. Thanks to the many experts who provided critical feedback and great ideas: Richard Muller, Mike Moriarty, Stephen Smith, Rick Casler, Babak Parviz, David Smith, Michael Czech, Jason Dickinson, Richard Obousy, Jose Maciel Natario, Matthew Andrews, Sangho Park, and Gabor Forgacs. Thanks to Adam Rogers, for assigning the realistic version of this story, plus Mr. Brown, Sergeant Dyer, and Skloot for early endorsements. Thanks to Harry Campbell for his wonderful illustrations. Ken Wright, for believing in the project, providing enormously helpful editorial guidance along the way, and, of course, finding the right publisher. Everyone at Bloomsbury, including Jenny Miyasaki and Sara Mercurio, and especially Ben Adams, a truly smart and funny editor, for helping me shape and refine the whole thing, and for adding some really choice one-liners.

A Note on the Author

GREGORY MONE is a contributing editor at *Popular Science* magazine. His feature articles have appeared in *Wired, Discover, Women's Health,* and *National Geographic Adventure,* as well as *The Best American Science Writing 2007.* He is also the author of the novel *The Wages of Genius* and lives in Massachusetts with his wife and two children.